Scrapbooking Techniques
Inking

Scrapbooking Techniques
Inking

Carol Heppner

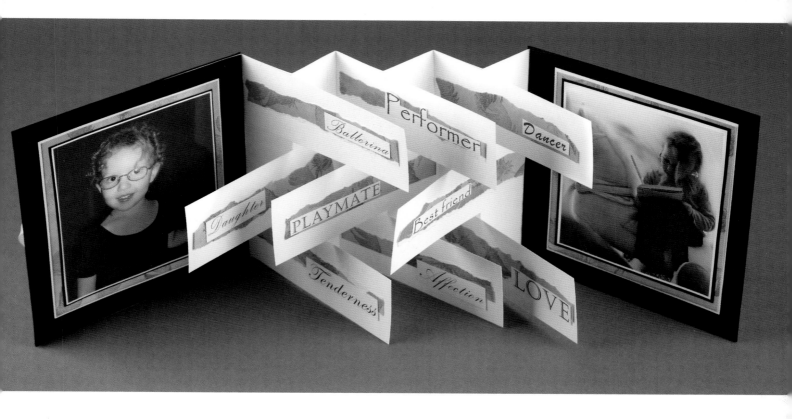

Sterling Publishing Co., Inc. New York
A Sterling/Chapelle Book

Chapelle, Ltd.
P.O. Box 9252, Ogden, UT 84409
(801) 621-2777 • (801) 621-2788 Fax
e-mail: chapelle@chapelleltd.com
Web site: www.chapelleltd.com

Library of Congress Cataloging-in-Publication Data

Heppner, Carol.
  Scrapbooking technique : inking / Carol Heppner.
    p. cm.
  Includes index.
  ISBN-13: 978-1-4027-2646-0
  ISBN-10: 1-4027-2646-5
  1. Photograph albums. 2. Scrapbooks. 3. Inking (Printing) 4.
Embossing
(Printing) 5. Rubber stamp printing. I. Title.
  TR501.H47 2006
  745.593--dc22

                                                                    2005032099

10 9 8 7 6 5 4 3 2 1
Published by Sterling Publishing Co., Inc.
387 Park Avenue South, New York, NY 10016
©2006 by Carol Heppner
Distributed in Canada by Sterling Publishing
c/o Canadian Manda Group, 165 Dufferin Street
Toronto, Ontario, Canada M6K 3H6
Distributed in the United Kingdom by GMC Distribution Services,
Castle Place, 166 High Street, Lewes, East Sussex, England BN7 1XU
Distributed in Australia by Capricorn Link (Australia) Pty. Ltd.
P.O. Box 704, Windsor, NSW 2756, Australia
Printed and Bound in China
All Rights Reserved

Sterling ISBN-13: 978-1-4027-2646-0
        ISBN-10: 1-4027-2646-5

   For information about custom editions, special sales, premium and corporate purchases, please contact Sterling Special Sales Department at 800-805-5489 or specialsales@sterlingpub.com.

Table of Contents

Introduction

Scrapbooking is a fun way to preserve memories and share experiences with your family, friends, and loved ones. How you put together a scrapbook page says a lot about your subject as well as your artistic style. Most people like to make a project that looks good, yet they want to do it relatively quickly and have some fun along the way.

This book will show you how to use polyester fiberfill with ink to create great background papers that you can use in scrapbooks. Yes, polyester fiberfill—the stuffing in your pillows—is a great tool to apply inks to scrapbook paper. It allows for effortless application on all sizes of papers with great results. The inking techniques described in this book are not limited to just scrapbooking, however. When you create large pieces of inked paper, your leftovers can serve as a "supply" for many different paper projects.

Let these scrapbook pages inspire you to add your own style. Alter colors to change the look of the background page, or use rubber stamps and embossing powders to add style and elegance. If you do not have the exact rubber stamp image that is used in this book, look for a rubber stamp in a similar shape. You can also substitute stickers or collage elements with a similar shape and color.

This book will provide all the things you need to know to get started making great scrapbook pages. As you read and learn the techniques, you are always encouraged to apply your style, your originality, and your personality. Your scrapbooks will be works of accomplishment—something that you will cherish for years to come.

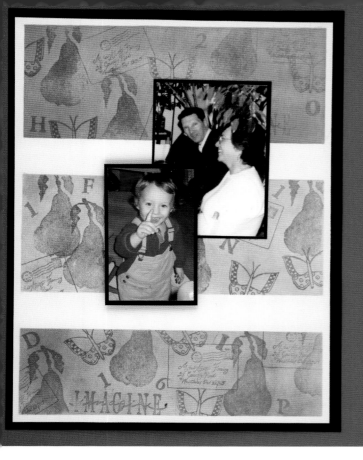

HOPE LIFE LIVING DIG IMAGINE

Spadafora Reunion

19 53

ARCHBALD

Christmas Card Ends 46-Year Separation

ARCHBALD—A Christmas card received by John Petrone, 230 South Main St., from John Spatafore of Detroit, Mich., resulted in a happy reunion Sunday night between Mr. Petrone's aged mother and her brother whom she had not seen or heard from in 46 years.

The name Spatfore was unfamiliar to Mr. Petrone and when he received the card he took it to his mother, Mrs. Angeline Petrone, 83, of 404 Ridge St. Mrs. Petrone said she had a brother by that name but added "I have not heard from him for 46 years and do not know whether he is dead or alive."

At the time Joseph Petrone, another son of Mrs. Petrone, who is employed in Bridgeport, Conn., was spending the holidays at his mother's home. He put in a telephone call to Detroit and through the aid of an operator there located Mr. Spatfore and talked with his long unheard from uncle for the first time.

Arrangements were made for Mr. Spatfore, who is 71, to fly here. He arrived at Avoca Airport Sunday night and was met by his nephews. A reunion followed at Mrs. Petrone's home.

Present were Mrs. Petrone, Mr. Spatfore, Mr. and Mrs. John Petrone and their children, Mr. and Mrs. Anthony Petrone, Mr. and Mrs. Edward Maichelitis, Betty, Delores, Shirley, Joan, Marie, John Jr. and James Maichelitis, all of Archbald; Mr. and Mrs. Michael Work of Olyphant and Mr. and Mrs. Joseph Petrone of Bridgeport.

Mr. Spatfore expects to remain here for a week and will then return to his home in Detroit.

1930

SCHOOL DAYS

1935

The Basics

This chapter provides the basic foundation for the papers you ink and the scrapbook projects you compose. The first section tells you about the various inks on the market and which types to choose for your artwork. The section on ink techniques and rubber stamping contains information about different applications of the polyester fiberfill inking technique. For example, you can use masking tape or a torn piece of paper to create unique patterns on the page. We will also look at the role of rubber stamps and powders in the scrapbook page. The projects that follow show how these techniques can complement your photographs and other ephemera. For instance, the wavy edge of the torn paper is a natural with ocean motifs, and aged paper works well with old black-and-white photographs. Experiment and have fun.

Understanding Inks and Color

When you take a trip to the ink pad aisle of your local craft store, you might be thinking about what colors to use in your project. Color is just one thing to consider, however. There are many different types of ink on the market, and knowing their attributes will help you find the right ink for your project.

Both the ink and the paper in your scrapbook should be fade resistant and acid free so that your pages will last a long time. Your projects are about preserving memories, after all!

Types of Inks

Permanent Dye Inks

Permanent dye inks are transparent and quick drying. These inks are made with a fade-resistant dye that is acid free. They are waterproof, and they will not smear when you apply other inks over them. Permanent dye inks are typically called archival inks.

Pigment Inks

Pigment inks are glycerin-based. The thicker and opaque pigment inks stay wet much longer than dye inks, which makes pigment inks perfect to use with embossing powders and metallic powders. Some pigment inks will dry on their own, but others will not dry without being heat set or dusted with embossing or metallic powders. It is important to read the back of the ink pad case to know the ink's characteristics. Pigment inks will not fade over time.

Water-based Dye Inks

Water-based dye inks are transparent, quick drying, and acid free. This ink smears with water, and the ink will rewet when other inks are placed on top of it. Water-based dye ink fades over time, making it a poor choice for scrapbook projects. A spray fixative can help prevent fading and make them more resistant to smearing and rewetting. However, permanent dye inks are favored for scrapbook projects.

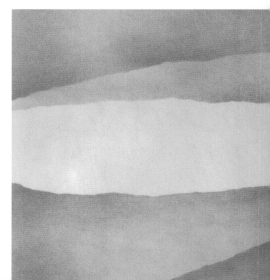

Ink Techniques and Rubber Stamping Guide

Although inks can be applied in a variety of ways—from brayers to stipple brushes—most techniques lack "user friendliness" and consistency. You want to attain a sharp, professional look to your pages, but you want to do it quickly and easily.

The answer is as close as a bag of fiberfill. Polyester fiberfill provides an excellent, consistent, quick way to apply inks to background papers used in scrapbooking. It can be found in the sewing areas of craft stores.

Inking Basics

It is important to make sure that the fiberfill you use is made of polyester. Since polyester is less absorbent than other materials, like sponges, it allows the ink to sit on the surface of the fibers and is a great substance to transfer ink. Tear pieces from the "bulk" of the fiberfill to use as your inking tool. The size of the piece you use will depend on the area you need to cover. Additionally, you will need to use a separate piece of fiberfill for each type or color of ink that you use.

Unless you love having your fingers a bright shade of pink, it is a good idea to wear latex or rubber gloves. Always keep a damp cloth at your work surface. The gloves will pick up the ink and can transfer it to other surfaces, so be certain to wipe your gloved hand when you are finished working with each color.

Inks are transparent. When using more than one color, apply the lightest color first. Apply the darkest color last. Once the dark ink is on the paper, you cannot lighten it with lighter ink. Also, keep in mind that applying the darkest color to the edges of the paper will produce a nice defined edge.

The following sections show different ink techniques that you can use to create scrapbook pages.

Solid Color

Rub a golf-ball-sized piece of polyester fiberfill over the ink pad. Starting at the edge of the paper, rub the ink-filled polyester fiberfill in a circular motion over the paper (Fig. 1). Continue transferring the ink onto the paper until the paper is covered (Fig. 2).

Fig. 1

Fig. 2

Monochromatic Shades

Select ink pads in light, medium, and dark shades of the same color. Rub a golf-ball-sized piece of polyester fiberfill over the light-colored ink pad. In a circular motion, apply the ink-filled polyester fiberfill over the desired area of the paper (Fig. 3). Rub a second piece of polyester fiberfill over the medium-colored ink and lightly apply it over the edges of the light-colored ink on the paper (Fig. 4). Rub a third piece of polyester fiberfill over the dark-colored ink and lightly apply it over the desired edges of the medium-colored ink on the paper (Fig. 5).

Complementary Multicolor

Select 2–4 coordinating ink pads. Rub a golf-ball-sized piece of polyester fiberfill over the light-colored ink pad. Apply this color over the desired area (Fig. 6). Rub a second piece of polyester fiberfill over the next color of ink. Apply the second color to the scrapbook paper (Fig. 7). Apply the remaining colors to the paper until you have completed the design (Fig. 8).

Fig. 6

Fig. 3

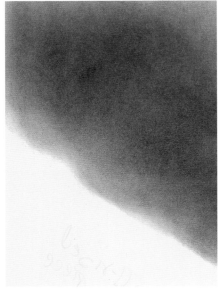

Fig. 4

Fig. 7

Fig. 5

Fig. 8

Masking Tape Techniques

Masking tape is an easy way to define areas of color, maintain the white of the paper, and create neat designs. It is a great tool to maintain crisp white borders. While low-tack masking tape is more expensive, it is easier to remove and there is less chance of tearing the paper.

Low-tack masking tape comes in one standard size. Higher-tack tapes come in varying widths. There are a few tricks to making higher-tack tapes less tacky. One way is to place the cut piece of tape on a piece of fabric, then remove the tape from the fabric. Repeat at least three times. Then apply the "conditioned" tape to the scrapbook paper.

You can also use an embossing heat tool to soften the adhesive of the masking tape as you remove it. Make certain you do not apply a great deal of heat or it will transfer the adhesive to the scrapbook paper.

When removing masking tape, start by lifting the corner closest to you. Gently and slowly pull the tape away from you; this reduces the chance of tearing the paper. Also, if the tape is applied along an edge of the paper, pull the tape toward rather than away from the edge to reduce tearing. If you find that the tape sticks to the paper, slightly heat it with the embossing heat tool.

Using Masking Tape to Enclose an Area

Apply low-tack or conditioned masking tape around all four sides of the paper (Fig. 9). Rub a golf-ball-sized piece of polyester fiberfill over the ink pad and apply the ink to the paper in a circular motion. Apply the heaviest coat of color near the edges of the masking tape (Fig. 10). Carefully remove the masking tape (Fig. 11).

Fig. 9

Fig. 10

Fig. 11

Using Masking Tape to Maintain the White of the Paper

Apply low-tack masking tape on the areas of the paper you want to remain white (Fig. 12). Rub a golf-ball-sized piece of polyester fiberfill over the ink pad and apply the ink to the paper in a circular motion. Apply the heaviest coat of color near the edges of the masking tape (Fig. 13). Carefully remove the masking tape (Fig. 14).

Using Masking Tape to Define Darker Areas of Color

Apply low-tack masking tape on the areas of the paper you want to remain white. Rub a golf-ball-sized piece of polyester fiberfill over the ink pad and apply the ink to the paper in a circular motion (Fig. 15). Place pieces of masking tape over desired areas of the paper (Fig. 16). Apply darker ink to center of the paper. Carefully remove the masking tape (Fig. 17).

Fig. 15

Fig. 12

Fig. 13

Fig. 16

Fig. 14

Fig. 17

Torn or Cut Paper Technique

You can tear a strip of paper in half to use the ragged edge, use regular scissors to cut a patterned edge, or use decorative-edged scissors to cut a patterned edge to act as a stencil. Whatever you use, you will have hours of fun coming up with new patterns for your background paper.

To create a torn-paper look, tear a strip of paper in half. Place it on the scrapbook paper. Using polyester fiberfill, apply ink to the paper along the edge of the torn paper (Fig. 18). Slightly move the torn paper down the scrapbook paper. Apply a second coat of ink (Fig. 19). Remove the torn paper and use polyester fiberfill to apply a soft coat of ink over the entire background paper (Fig. 20). Rotate the background paper 180º and repeat the above steps (Fig. 21).

Fig. 18

Fig. 19

Fig. 20

Fig. 21

Aging Paper

Sometimes a scrapbook project or page calls for paper to look "aged." Aged paper and old photographs go hand in hand in scrapbooks. It is simple enough to give paper that tea-stained look by using light tan and light brown inks.

Stamped images, scrapbooking tags, even background paper can be aged. If you do any heritage scrapbooking, you will love this technique. Look for inks that are designed to work with heritage scrapbooking.

To age paper, tear one or two corners of the paper. Fold corners or areas of the paper that you want to look creased. Using polyester fiberfill, apply light tan ink to the entire paper. Randomly apply old-paper-colored (very light brown-green) ink to parts of the paper. Apply tea-stain-colored ink over the creases. Apply the same ink to the edges of the paper. Apply dark brown ink to the torn edges of the paper (Figs. 22 and 23).

Stencils

There are so many wonderful stencils that can be applied to scrapbooking. You can create a large sheet of one design and use it on several projects. When working with a full sheet of scrapbook paper to trace a stencil for a motif, always use the paper conservatively so that remaining excess paper can be used later.

To create one design, use low-tack masking tape to secure the stencil to your scrapbook paper. Use a marble-sized piece of fiberfill to apply each color over the stencil. Remove the stencil from the paper. If desired, apply a light coat of ink over the stenciled area (Fig. 24).

Rubber Stamps

Rubber stamps are a wonderful way to give texture to scrapbook papers (Fig. 25). You can also stamp an image, color it with inks or colored pencils, and use it as an embellishment on your papers. When using a full sheet of scrapbook paper to rubber-stamp an image, always use the paper conservatively so that remaining excess paper can be used later.

For best results, follow these steps: Tap the rubber stamp onto the ink pad. If the rubber stamp is large, you can place it upside down on a table and tap the ink pad onto the rubber stamp. Make sure the ink has covered the entire image. Place the image onto paper and apply pressure to the rubber-stamp mount. Do not rock or slide the rubber stamp. Gently lift the rubber stamp from the paper.

Fig. 24

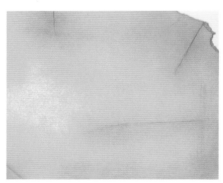

Fig. 22

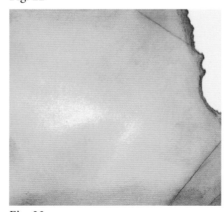

Fig. 23

Fig. 25

Powders

Powders offer a way to add eye-catching detail to any project. There are two types of powders that are used with rubber stamps: embossing powders and pigment powders.

Embossing Powders

There are many embossing powders on the market. They come in the same range of colors as inks. Some companies even match their embossing powders to their ink colors.

Despite their many names, there are three basic consistency types of embossing powders: ultrathin, regular, and ultrathick. Because each manufacturer will have their own names for their lines of embossing powders, it is a good idea to read the fine print on each container.

Ultrathin embossing powders produce a very fine line and work well with detailed text and stamps. Ultra-thin powders are sometimes referred to as "detailed embossing powders." Ultra-thick embossing powders are used for coating large areas. Ultrathick powders are great for making wearable pins and other embellishments. All other embossing powders fall in the normal category. They work well with most stamped images (Fig. 26).

Embossing powders grab onto wet areas of the paper, which is why pigment ink is best for use with embossing powder. However, static cling and oils from your hand will also cause the powder to cling to the paper. If you lightly dust talc-free baby powder over the paper before stamping, the embossing powder will stick only to the ink.

Embossing Heat Tool

The embossing heat tool is used to quickly melt embossing powders. It produces a concentrated stream of intense heat. Blow driers do not achieve the same level of heat, and the airflow is too diffused. The tip of the embossing heat tool can become quite hot. Even though there is a power switch on your embossing heat tool, never leave the tool plugged in when you are not using it. It is just like any electrical device, so it is important to follow the safety guidelines on the package.

Embossing Powder Instructions

Dust the entire scrapbook paper with talc-free baby powder. Tap the rubber stamp onto a pigment ink pad, then stamp the image onto powdered paper. Sprinkle embossing powder over the wet impression. Shake off the excess powder onto a folded piece of paper, then return the excess powder to its jar. Hold the heat tool about 3" from the paper and slowly move the heat over the powder until it becomes shiny. Do not overheat the embossing powder as overheating causes the powder to become flat and discolored. Let the powder cool.

Pigment Powders

Pigment powders are an easy way to add a bit of soft shine to the page. They can be dusted over embossing inks. Pigment powders come in a wide range of colors and finishes. They produce a metallic sheen, pearlescent shimmer, or various faux finishes (Fig. 27). They are fade resistant and acid free.

Some ink companies make pigment powders that do not need to be sealed. However, all pigment powders can be sealed with a workable spray fixative.

Pigment powders can be mixed with clear embossing powder to create your own custom embossing powder. You can also experiment using different pigment ink colors with powder colors.

Pigment Powder Instructions

Dust the entire scrapbook paper with talc-free baby powder. Tap the rubber stamp onto a pigment ink pad, then stamp the image onto powdered paper. With a soft brush, dust a small amount of the pigment powder over the inked image. It is easier to apply more powder than it is to remove excess powder. Use a clean, dry, soft brush to remove the excess powder. Be certain to do this lightly so as to not smear the ink or remove too much powder. Carefully clean the area with a ball of polyester fiberfill. Seal the image with a spray fixative.

Fig. 26

Fig. 27

Waiting for the White Rabbit

Materials

- 4" x 9¾" piece of white scrapbook paper
- 8½" x 11" sheets of white scrapbook paper (2)
- 12"-square sheets of white scrapbook paper (2)
- Adhesive foam dots
- Archival paper glue
- Butterfly rubber stamp
- Craft scissors
- Ink in cobalt blue
- Large photograph
- Leaf rubber stamp
- Polyester fiberfill
- Ruler
- Small square photographs (3)

Instructions

1. Use polyester fiberfill to apply ink to a 12"-square paper. Randomly stamp the leaf pattern over the inked paper.

2. Cut the paper to 10" square. Glue the 10"-square paper to the remaining 12"-square paper.

3. Glue the 4" x 9¾" paper to the bottom of the inked paper.

4. Glue photographs to an 8½" x 11" paper. Trim the paper to slightly larger than the photographs.

5. Using foam dots, attach the large photograph to the upper part of the inked paper. Attach the remaining photographs to the 4" x 9¾" paper.

6. Stamp three butterfly images onto the remaining 8½" x 11" paper. Cut out the butterflies and glue them near the large photograph.

Family Name

Materials

- 8"-square piece of white scrapbook paper
- 8¼" x 10" piece of black scrapbook paper
- 8½" x 11" sheet of black scrapbook paper
- 8½" x 11" sheet of white scrapbook paper
- 10½"-square piece of white scrapbook paper
- 11"-square piece of white scrapbook paper
- 12"-square sheet of white scrapbook paper
- Adhesive foam dots
- Archival paper glue
- Computer and printer
- Craft scissors
- Inks in mustard yellow, sepia, and terra-cotta
- Large photograph
- Polyester fiberfill
- Small photograph

Pasquale, Andrea, Gianmarco

Instructions

1. Use polyester fiberfill to apply mustard yellow ink to the top third of the 8"-square paper. Apply terra-cotta ink to the center area of the paper. Apply sepia ink to the bottom third of the paper.

2. Apply mustard yellow ink to the edges of the 11"-square paper.

3. Center and glue the mustard-yellow-edged paper to the 12"-square paper.

4. Glue the 10½"-square paper over the mustard-yellow-edged paper, allowing the mustard yellow paper to act as a border.

5. Center and glue the 8¼" x 10" black paper onto the 10½"-square white paper. Print white text on a black background onto the 8½" x 11" white paper. Cut the strip of text from the paper. Glue the text strip onto the left-hand side of the black paper. Glue the tricolored paper onto the right-hand side of the black paper.

6. Glue the large and small photographs to the 8½" x 11" black paper. Trim the black paper to slightly larger than the photographs.

7. Glue the larger photograph to the center of the tricolored paper. Using foam dots, attach the smaller photograph slightly below the larger photograph.

Easy Rider

Materials

- 8½" x 11" sheets of white scrapbook paper (2)
- 11"-square piece of white scrapbook paper
- 12"-square sheets of white scrapbook paper (2)
- Archival paper glue
- Beaded wire (optional)
- Boot rubber stamp
- Clear gel craft glue
- Computer and printer, or alphabet rubber stamps and black ink
- Craft scissors
- Horse rubber stamp
- Inks in meadow green, sepia, and true blue
- Large photograph
- Miniature gardening tool (optional)
- Miniature tassel (optional)
- Needle and white thread
- Polyester fiberfill
- Small photographs (3)

Instructions

1. Use polyester fiberfill to apply true blue ink to the top quarter of the 11"-square paper. Apply meadow green ink to the center of the paper. Apply sepia ink to the bottom quarter of the paper.

2. Cut a 12"-square paper to slightly larger than the large photograph. Apply true blue ink to the edges of the paper. Use archival paper glue to adhere the photograph to the true blue paper.

3. Stamp the horse with sepia ink and the boot with true blue ink onto an 8½" x 11" paper. Cut out the horse and boot.

4. Print text onto the remaining 8½" x 11" paper so that each letter can be cut into 1" squares. Cut out the letter squares.

5. Glue the tricolored paper to the remaining 12"-square sheet paper.

6. Glue the horse to the upper-left corner of the paper. Glue the boot to the lower-right corner of the paper.

7. Glue the large photograph to the center of the paper. Use white thread to string the letter squares together. Arrange the text around the photograph. Glue the three smaller photographs to the lower-left corner.

8. If desired, embellish with a miniature gardening tool wrapped with beads. Use clear gel craft glue to adhere a miniature tassel to the end of the tool. Glue the tool below the photograph.

Easy

Rider

A Midweek Escape

Materials

- 8½" x 11" sheet of white scrapbook paper
- 11"-square piece of white scrapbook paper
- 12"-square sheets of white scrapbook paper (2)
- Adhesive foam dots
- Archival paper glue
- Computer and printer, or marker
- Craft scissors
- Inks in banana yellow, cobalt blue, and true blue
- Large photograph
- Leaf rubber stamp
- Polyester fiberfill

Instructions

1. Use polyester fiberfill to apply true blue ink to the 11"-square paper. Apply cobalt blue ink around the four edges of the paper. Using the cobalt blue ink, randomly stamp the leaf image on the left-hand side and the bottom part of the inked paper.

2. Cut a 12"-square paper to slightly larger than the photograph. Apply cobalt blue ink to the edges of the paper. Glue the photograph to the cobalt paper.

3. Center and print text onto the 8½" x 11" paper. *Note: You can also handwrite your text on the paper, but you must make sure to use waterproof ink.* Tear a rectangle around the text, including about 6" above. Apply banana yellow ink over the paper, making certain the ink is applied heavier on the edges.

4. Using the cobalt blue ink pad, stamp three leaves onto excess white scrapbook paper. Apply true blue ink to the leaves. Cut out the leaves. Glue the leaves above the text on the yellow paper.

5. Glue the cobalt paper to the remaining 12"-square sheet of white scrapbook paper.

6. Glue the yellow piece to the cobalt paper, tilting it slightly to the right.

7. Use foam dots to attach the photograph to the left-hand side of the larger blue paper. Overlap the lower-right corner of the photograph with the lower corner of the yellow piece.

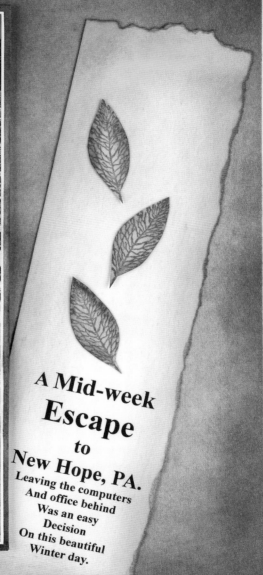

A Mid-week
Escape
to
New Hope, PA.
Leaving the computers
And office behind
Was an easy
Decision
On this beautiful
Winter day.

Memorial Day Parade
Eynon, PA

Edward Marchelitis
Paul Heppner, Son-in Law
Gina Gifford, Granddaughter

Memorial Day Parade

Materials

- 7½" x 10" piece of white scrapbook paper
- 8½" x 11" sheets of white scrapbook paper (2)
- 10"-square piece of white scrapbook paper
- 12"-square sheet of white scrapbook paper
- Archival paper glue
- Clock face or other circular rubber stamp
- Computer and printer
- Craft scissors
- Inks in banana yellow and mustard yellow
- Photographs (3)
- Polyester fiberfill

Instructions

1. Use polyester fiberfill to apply banana yellow ink to the 10"-square paper.

2. Apply mustard yellow ink to the 7½" x 10" paper. Randomly stamp the clock image with mustard yellow ink onto the entire paper.

3. Print text onto an 8½" x 11" paper. Cut the text from the paper.

4. Glue the banana yellow background paper to the 12"-square paper.

5. Glue the mustard yellow paper over the banana yellow background, tilting it to the left.

6. Glue photographs to the remaining 8½" x 11" paper. Trim paper to slightly larger than the photographs. Glue photographs and text as desired onto the mustard yellow paper.

A Study in Gray

Materials

- ¼" and ½" hole punches
- 3" x 5" piece of white scrapbook paper
- 7½" x 10" piece of white scrapbook paper
- 8½" x 11" sheet of black scrapbook paper
- 8½" x 11" sheet of white scrapbook paper
- Adhesive foam dots
- Archival paper glue
- Craft scissors
- Inks in black and crimson red
- Photograph
- Polyester fiberfill

Instructions

1. Use polyester fiberfill to lightly apply black ink to the 7½" x 10" paper. Apply the ink more heavily to the upper part of the paper. Create three lines on the upper part of the paper by applying more ink in that area with the polyester fiberfill.

2. Apply crimson red ink to the 3" x 5" paper. Punch three holes with the ½" hole punch and three with the ¼" hole punch.

3. Glue the background paper to the 8½" x 11" sheet of white scrapbook paper.

4. Cut a piece from the 8½" x 11" black paper to slightly larger than the photograph. Glue the photograph to the paper. Using foam dots, attach the photograph to the center of the paper. Glue the three larger circles to the bottom of the page. Glue the smaller circles to the top of the page.

Puppy Love

Materials

- ¼" hole punch
- 6½" x 11" piece of white scrapbook paper
- 8½" x 11" sheets of white scrapbook paper (3)
- 12"-square sheet of white scrapbook paper
- Adhesive foam dots
- Archival paper glue
- Computer and printer
- Craft scissors
- Eyelet setter
- Flower rubber stamp
- Heart stencils in 3 different sizes
- Inks in carnation pink and true blue
- Jump rings (2)
- Pencil
- Photographs (3)
- Polyester fiberfill
- Ruler
- Silver heart charms (2)
- White eyelets (2)
- White thread

Instructions

1. Use polyester fiberfill to apply carnation pink ink to the 6½" x 11" paper. Stamp a random flower pattern with carnation pink ink onto the paper.

2. Apply true blue ink to an 8½" x 11" paper. Cut the paper into two rectangles, one measuring 1" x 2½" and one measuring 2½" x 10". Punch three circles from the remaining blue paper, then cut a stem and two small leaves from the remaining blue paper.

3. Stamp a flower with carnation pink ink onto an 8½" x 11" paper, then trace three hearts of different sizes onto the paper. Apply carnation pink ink to the hearts. Cut out the flower and the hearts. Glue the hearts to excess white scrapbook paper. Trim the white paper to slightly larger than the hearts. Punch two holes each in the two smaller hearts. Thread white thread through the holes and tie in a knot.

4. Print text onto the remaining 8½" x 11" paper. Cut the text from the paper. Using the eyelet setter, attach eyelets to each end of the text. Use jump rings to attach the hearts to the eyelets.

5. Glue the flower-patterned paper to the bottom half of the 12"-square paper.

6. Glue the large true blue rectangle slightly above the pink flower paper. Glue the text over the lower part of the true blue paper.

7. Glue a photograph above the text. Glue the small rectangle to the upper-left corner. Use foam dots to attach the largest heart over the rectangles. Glue the three blue dots near the top of the heart. Glue the two smaller hearts on the opposite side of the photograph.

8. Glue two photographs to the bottom of the page. Use foam dots to attach the flower between the photographs. Glue the stem and leaves in place.

Puppy Love

Beautiful *Colors*

Beautiful Colors

Materials

- ⅛" x 12" strip of white scrapbook paper
- 8½" x 11" sheets of white scrapbook paper (2)
- Archival paper glue
- Button
- Clear gel craft glue
- Craft scissors
- Different-sized photographs (3)
- Flat bead
- Green ribbon
- Handmade or purchased wire embellishment
- Inks in aqua, dark green, meadow green, and purple
- Polyester fiberfill
- Vellum paper with text

Instructions

1. Use polyester fiberfill to apply purple ink to the upper-left side of an 8½" x 11" paper. Apply aqua ink to the upper-right side of the scrapbook paper. Apply meadow green ink to the lower section of the scrapbook paper.

2. Use the archival paper glue to adhere the largest photograph to the bottom-right side of the paper. Glue the two smaller photographs to the upper-left corner.

3. Apply dark green ink to the ⅛" x 12" strip. Cut the strip into two portions. Glue one horizontally and one vertically onto the scrapbook page in the desired location.

4. Cut three small squares from the remaining 8½" x 11" paper. Apply meadow green ink to each square. Tilt two squares into diamond shapes and glue to the left-hand side of the page.

5. Tilt remaining square into a diamond shape and glue to the top of the tripatterned paper. Glue vellum text onto the diamond shape. Use clear gel craft glue to adhere the flat bead to the right-hand side of the diamond shape.

6. Glue the wire embellishment, button, and green ribbon to the scrapbook page.

Heartwarming

Materials

- 8½" x 11" sheet of white scrapbook paper
- Adhesive foam dots
- Archival paper glue
- Bracelet fragment
- Clear gel craft glue
- Flat bead
- Inks in carnation pink, mustard yellow, and sepia
- Large photograph
- Low-tack masking tape
- Multicolored thread
- Polyester fiberfill
- Vellum paper with text
- Watercolor paper

Instructions

1. Use masking tape to protect the edges of the 8½" x 11" paper. Use polyester fiberfill to apply mustard yellow ink to the top half of the paper. Apply carnation pink ink to the lower half of the paper. Apply sepia ink to the edges near the tape. Slowly remove the tape from the paper.

2. Use archival paper glue to adhere the photograph slightly above the center of the paper.

3. Tear a strip from watercolor paper to desired size. Use clear gel craft glue to adhere two pieces of thread to the right-hand side of the strip. Use archival paper glue to adhere the vellum text onto the center of the strip, tilting it slightly. Use clear gel craft glue to adhere the bracelet fragment across the paper, going over the thread and the vellum text.

4. Tear a shorter strip from watercolor paper to approximately the same width as the larger strip. Glue a piece of thread and a bead to the paper. Use foam dots to attach the smaller strip over the end of the larger strip. Use foam dots to attach the entire piece to the scrapbook page.

Our Cabin

Materials

- 8½" x 11" sheet of white scrapbook paper
- Archival paper glue
- Different-sized photographs (2)
- Inks in meadow green and pesto green
- Low-tack masking tape
- Poem sticker
- Polyester fiberfill
- Vellum paper with text (2)

Instructions

1. Apply masking tape to all four edges of the 8½" x 11" paper to create a ¼" border. Use polyester fiberfill to lightly apply meadow green ink to the paper. Apply the ink more heavily on some areas of the paper. Apply pesto green ink over the meadow green paper. Apply the ink more heavily on some areas of the paper. Reapply the pesto green ink around the edges of the paper.

2. Carefully remove the tape.

3. Glue the larger photograph to the page as desired. Add the poem sticker to the right-hand side of the page. Glue the smaller photograph to the left-hand side of the scrapbook page. Glue the vellum text to the page.

The Park

Materials

- ¼" hole punch
- 8½" x 11" sheet of black scrapbook paper
- 8½" x 11" sheets of white scrapbook paper (2)
- Archival paper glue
- Craft knife
- Craft scissors
- Cutting mat
- Fern leaf rubber stamp
- Inks in cobalt blue, meadow green, and true blue
- Low-tack masking tape
- Pencil
- Photograph
- Polyester fiberfill
- Ruler
- Straight pin

Instructions

1. Place masking tape around the edge of an 8½" x 11" white paper to create a ¼" border. Using true blue ink, stamp the leaf image randomly over the paper.

2. Use polyester fiberfill to apply true blue ink over the stamp design. Apply meadow green ink to the edges of the paper.

3. Cut a 5" x 7" piece from a corner of the remaining 8½" x 11" white paper. Place photograph in the center of the 5" x 7" paper. Use a straight pin to pierce a small hole to mark the four corners of the photograph on the rectangle. Remove the photograph from the paper. Draw a line to connect the four holes. On a cutting mat, cut along the lines with the craft knife.

4. Apply true blue ink over the frame. Apply cobalt blue ink to the inside and outside edges of the paper. Glue the frame to the photograph.

5. Cut excess white scrapbook paper to slightly larger than the frame. Using foam dots, attach the framed photograph to the white paper.

6. Cut a corner from the 8½" x 11" black paper to 7½" square. Glue the black square to the upper part of the leaf-patterned paper. Glue the framed photograph to the upper part of the black square.

7. Punch four holes from excess black paper. Glue the circles to the four corners.

8. Use the true blue ink to stamp the leaf image onto excess white scrapbook paper. Cut out the leaf, leaving a white border. Glue the leaf to the lower part of the black paper.

Sweet Pink

Materials

- ¼" hole punch
- 8½" x 11" sheets of white scrapbook paper (3)
- 12"-square sheets of white scrapbook paper (3)
- Archival paper glue
- Beaded pearl trim
- Computer and printer
- Craft scissors
- Embossing heat tool

- Flower paper punch
- Inks in carnation pink and meadow green
- Large floral stencil
- Low-tack masking tape
- Oval paper punch
- Polyester fiberfill
- Quilter's masking tape
- Round photograph
- Ruler
- Tag paper punch, or white tags

Instructions

1. Use masking tape to secure the floral stencil to a 12"-square paper. Use polyester fiberfill to slowly rub carnation pink ink over the stencil. Cut the paper to 5" x 10".

2. Use quilter's masking tape to create a striped pattern on a second 12"-square paper. Leave a ¼" space between each piece of masking tape. Apply carnation pink ink to the exposed areas of the paper. Place the floral stencil over the paper. Use polyester fiberfill to slowly rub the carnation pink ink over the stencil. Remove the stencil. Use the embossing heat tool to lightly apply heat to the masking tape. Slowly remove the tape from the paper. Cut the paper to 5" x 10".

3. Apply meadow green ink to an 8½" x 11" paper. Punch out 14 flowers. Apply carnation pink ink to a second 8½" x 11" paper. Punch out about three dozen circles and three dozen ovals from the carnation pink paper. Glue a carnation pink circle to the center of each flower.

4. Print out letters of photograph subject's name onto the remaining 8½" x 11" paper. Use a tag hole punch to cut out each letter. *Note: You can also print letters onto ready-made tags.*

5. Glue the flower stencil paper to the top of the remaining 12"-square paper, leaving a 1" border from the top and sides of the paper. Glue the striped paper to the bottom of the page, also leaving a 1" border from the bottom and side edges.

6. Place a dot of glue on the back of each green flower and adhere the flowers to the center of the paper. Glue the tags under the flower petals.

7. Glue the carnation pink circles and ovals in an alternating pattern around the edges of the stenciled floral paper. Choose one circle on each side and top in the alternating pattern and create a flower by adding four additional ovals around the circle.

8. Glue the photograph to the scrapbook page. Glue the beaded pearl trim around the photograph.

Savor Life

Materials

- ¼" hole punch
- 1½"-square piece of lace
- 1½"-square piece of watercolor paper
- 5" x 8" piece of white scrapbook paper
- 8½" x 11" sheets of white scrapbook paper (2)
- 12"-square sheet of white scrapbook paper
- Adhesive foam dots
- Archival paper glue
- Bead
- Button
- Clear gel craft glue
- Craft scissors
- Embossing heat tool
- Inks in pesto green and tea-stain brown
- Large alphabet stencil
- Low-tack masking tape
- Photograph
- Polyester fiberfill
- Quilter's masking tape
- Ribbon
- Ruler
- Typewriter alphabet stickers

Instructions

1. Use low-tack masking tape to create a ¼" border around the four edges of the 12"-square paper. Place a horizontal strip of low-tack masking tape 2"–3" from the top border. Use polyester fiberfill to lightly apply the pesto green ink to the area above the masking tape.

2. Place two vertical pieces of low-tack masking tape right next to each other on the left-hand side of the paper. Lightly apply pesto green ink to the lower-right exposed area of the paper. Remove the three pieces of tape. Lightly apply pesto green ink over the entire page.

3. To create the darker green vertical lines, cover the bottom edge of the upper-right pesto green box with low-tack masking tape to protect it. On the left-hand side of the page, place a horizontal strip of quilter's masking tape ⅛" from the masking tape border. Place a strip of low-tack masking tape ⅛" from the strip of quilter's masking tape. Apply pesto green ink heavily in the exposed areas. *Note: Do not remove the masking tape just yet.*

4. To create the darker green horizontal lines, place a strip of quilter's masking tape ⅛" from the horizontal piece of masking tape that is protecting the top of the page. Place a second strip of quilter's masking tape ⅛" from the first horizontal piece of tape. Place a strip of low-tack masking tape ⅛" from the second strip of tape. Apply pesto green ink heavily to the exposed areas. Lightly heat the tape with the embossing heat tool. Carefully remove all pieces of tape.

5. Apply tea-stain brown ink over the 5" x 8" paper in an uneven pattern. Cut an 8½" x 11" paper to slightly larger than the tea-stain brown paper. Apply tea-stain brown ink around the edges of the larger paper. *Note: Make sure the edges of this paper are darker than the first piece of paper.* Use archival paper glue to adhere the two pieces of paper together.

6. Punch a hole on the left-hand side of the paper and tie a ribbon in the hole.

7. Stencil text in the upper-left area of the background paper. Glue the tea-stain brown piece to the page.

8. Cut the remaining 8½" x 11" paper to slightly larger than the photograph. Apply tea-stain brown ink around the edges of the paper. Glue the photograph to the paper. Glue the matted photograph to the tea-stain brown piece on the page. Use foam dots to attach the typewriter alphabet stickers to the tea-stain brown piece.

9. Apply tea-stain brown ink to the 1½"-square paper. Use clear gel craft glue to adhere the lace and button over the square. Glue the bead to one corner of the square. Use foam dots to attach the embellishment to the scrapbook page.

SAVOR

LIFE

Cruising on the **Queen Mary**

The Queen's Shell Castle

Cruising on the Queen Mary

Materials

- 4" x 12" piece of scrap paper
- 8½" x 11" sheet of vellum paper
- 8½" x 11" sheets of white scrapbook paper (2)
- 12"-square sheet of white scrapbook paper
- Archival paper glue
- Craft scissors
- Different-sized photographs (3)
- Embossing heat tool
- Inks in aqua and cobalt blue
- Low-tack masking tape
- Miniature postcard rubber stamp
- Quilter's masking tape
- Scrap paper

Instructions

1. Apply low-tack masking tape around the edges of the 12"-square paper to create a 1" border. Place a second piece of low-tack masking tape about 8" from the top of the page. Cover the area below the masking tape with a piece of scrap paper to protect it from ink.

2. Cut a wave pattern along one edge of the 4" x 12" paper. Place the wave-patterned edge of the paper ½" from the top of the page. Use polyester fiberfill to apply cobalt blue ink to the area. Move the wave stencil down the page ½" and apply the ink again. Continue down the page in this manner. Remove the scrap paper from the bottom of the page.

3. Apply horizontal strips of quilter's masking tape to create a striped pattern on the bottom of the page.

Starting on the left-hand side, apply nine vertical strips of quilter's masking tape to create a grid pattern.

4. Apply cobalt blue ink over the exposed areas of the scrapbook paper. Lightly heat the masking tape with the embossing heat tool. Carefully remove all pieces of masking tape.

5. Use quilter's masking tape to create different-sized grid patterns on an 8½" x 11" paper. Apply aqua ink to the exposed areas of the paper. Lightly heat the masking tape with the embossing heat tool. Carefully remove all pieces of masking tape. Cut a large circle and a small circle from the paper.

6. Glue the large circle to the upper left of the page. Glue the small circle to the lower right of the page.

7. Glue the medium photograph to the upper-left area of the page, placing a portion over the larger circle. Glue the smallest photograph to the lower-left area of the page.

8. Cut the remaining 8½" x 11" paper to slightly larger than the largest photograph. Use polyester fiberfill to apply cobalt blue ink around the edges of the paper. Glue the photograph to the paper.

9. Cut a piece from vellum paper to slightly larger than the blue-edged paper. Glue the blue-edged paper to the vellum. Glue the entire piece to the right-hand side of the page, placing one corner over the smaller circle.

10. Stamp three miniature postcards onto excess white scrapbook paper using cobalt blue ink. Cut out the postcards and glue them to the upper-right area of the page.

Wild Horses

Materials

- 12"-square sheets of white scrapbook paper (4)
- Adhesive foam dots
- Archival paper glue
- Beaded pearl trim
- Clear gel craft glue
- Craft scissors
- Horse rubber stamp
- Inks in crimson red, latte, and sepia
- Miniature bricks
- Photograph
- Polyester fiberfill
- Ruler
- Scrap of lace

Instructions

1. Use sepia ink to stamp the horse image onto a 12"-square paper. Cut out the image. Use polyester fiberfill to apply sepia ink to the horse image. Place the horse image onto the left-hand side of a second 12"-square paper. Apply sepia ink over the edges of the horse image and on the scrapbook paper. Move the horse image to the right and repeat the process. Continue this process until the entire page is covered with a pattern. Cut the paper to approximately 9" square.

2. Cut a strip from excess white scrapbook paper. Apply crimson red ink to the strip. *Note: You will use this piece of scrapbook paper as a stencil.* Place the stencil on the upper-left side of a third 12"-square paper. Apply crimson red ink over the edges of the stencil and onto the page. Move the stencil to the right and repeat the process until the entire page is covered.

3. Cut a piece from the crimson patterned paper to about ¹⁄₂" larger all around than the photograph. Use archival paper glue to adhere the photograph onto the paper. Cut four long strips from the remaining crimson patterned paper.

4. Cut a piece from excess white scrapbook paper to slightly larger than the crimson patterned/matted photograph. Apply crimson red ink to the edges of the paper. Glue the crimson patterned paper onto the crimson-edged paper.

5. Glue the horse-patterned paper to the upper-right side of the remaining 12"-square paper. Use foam dots to attach the matted photograph to the center of the horse-patterned

paper. Glue two strips of crimson patterned paper to the left-hand side of the horse-patterned paper.

6. Glue the sepia horse image to the lower-left corner of the page. Stamp a horse in latte ink onto excess white scrapbook paper and cut out the image. Glue the latte horse over the sepia horse.

7. Glue the strip of solid crimson paper below the horse-patterned paper. Glue the two remaining crimson patterned strips below the solid crimson strip.

8. Use clear gel craft glue to adhere the beaded pearl trim around the photograph frame. Glue the scrap of lace below the right-hand side of the photograph. Glue the miniature bricks over the lace.

My Girl

Materials

- 2" x 4" piece of white scrapbook paper
- 8½" x 10" piece of vellum paper
- 12"-square sheet of white scrapbook paper
- Adhesive foam dots
- Archival paper glue
- Craft scissors
- Embossing heat tool
- Inks in cobalt blue and true blue
- Large photograph
- Low-tack masking tape
- Oval paper punch
- Quilter's masking tape
- Ruler
- Scrap paper
- Small photographs (3)
- Typewriter alphabet stickers

Instructions

1. Use low-tack masking tape to create a ¼" border around the four edges of the 12"-square paper.

2. Starting from the top, place an 8" piece of low-tack masking tape vertically on the paper approximately 2" from the left-hand side of the page. Starting from the left, place a 9" piece of masking tape horizontally approximately 2" from the top edge of the paper. Rotate the paper 180° and apply two more strips of masking tape in the same manner.

3. In the two "L" shaped areas of the scrapbook paper, create a diamond grid with quilter's masking tape. Use polyester fiberfill to apply true blue ink over the open areas of the grid. Randomly apply cobalt blue ink over the true blue ink.

4. Punch an oval into scrap paper to create a stencil. Use polyester fiberfill to stencil cobalt ink ovals in a few of the diamond shapes.

5. Apply true blue ink over the remaining open areas of the scrapbook paper. Apply cobalt blue ink around the edges of the masking tape.

6. Lightly heat the masking tape with the embossing heat tool. Carefully remove all pieces of masking tape.

7. Tear a piece of low-tack masking tape and place it in the center of the 2" x 4" paper. Apply true blue ink to the edges of the paper. Remove the masking tape. Apply the typewriter alphabet stickers to the paper.

8. Glue the 8½" x 10" vellum paper to the lower-left area of the page. Glue the large photograph to the center of the vellum paper. Attach the typewriter sticker tag and the smaller photographs to the scrapbook page, using foam dots.

MY GIRL

Spanish Tile

Materials

- 4" x 5" piece of black scrapbook paper
- 4" x 11" piece of black scrapbook paper
- 8½" x 11" sheet of white scrapbook paper
- 12"-square sheet of white scrapbook paper
- Adhesive foam dots
- Archival paper glue
- Circular map rubber stamp
- Clear gel craft glue
- Craft scissors
- Gold metallic pigment powder
- Inks in clear pigment, crimson red, latte, and sepia
- Low-tack masking tape
- Photograph
- Polyester fiberfill
- Polymer clay
- Raffia
- Tassel
- Text rubber stamp
- Thin-gauge wire
- White scrap paper
- White tags (3)
- White thread
- Wire and beads

Instructions

1. Use low-tack masking tape to create a 1" border around the 12"-square paper. Tear strips of masking tape and place them diagonally over the paper to create a rough-edged diamond pattern. Use polyester fiberfill to apply sepia ink over the exposed areas of the paper. Remove the diagonal masking tape. Lightly apply latte ink over the white areas of the paper.

2. Use pigment ink to randomly stamp the circular map on the 4" x 11" black paper. Dust with gold metallic powder. Use archival paper glue to adhere the black paper to the left side of the scrapbook page.

3. Use pigment ink to stamp the text image onto the 4" x 5" black paper. Dust the paper with gold metallic powder. Cut the 8½" x 11" white paper to slightly larger than the black text paper. Glue the black text paper to the white paper. Use foam dots to attach the black text piece to the 4" x 11" black paper.

4. Cut excess white paper to slightly larger than the photograph. Glue the photograph to the paper. Use foam dots to attach the matted photograph to the page.

5. Color white scrap paper with latte ink. Cut into three small strips. Glue each strip around a white tag. Use raffia to tie wire and beads to each tag. Thread white thread through wire and through tag openings. Use foam dots to attach the tags to the scrapbook page.

6. Shape polymer clay into a rectangle. Bake according to the polymer clay directions. Apply crimson red ink over the clay. Use crimson red ink to stamp text over the polymer clay. Wrap the clay with thin-gauge wire. Use clear gel craft glue to adhere a tassel to the back of the clay. Glue the clay embellishment to the scrapbook page.

Red Plaid

Materials

- 4" x 5" piece of vellum paper
- 7½" x 10" piece of white scrapbook paper
- 8½" x 11" sheets of black scrapbook paper (2)
- Archival paper glue
- Craft scissors
- Green ribbon
- Inks in crimson red, mustard yellow, pesto green, and true blue
- Low-tack masking tape
- Photograph
- Polyester fiberfill
- Quick-drying craft glue
- Star embellishment
- Vellum paper with text

Instructions

1. Use masking tape to create a ¼" border around the four edges of the 7½" x 10" paper. Place a vertical strip of tape ½" from the left-hand side of the tape border. Place a second strip of tape 1" from the first strip of tape. Place a third strip of tape ¾" from the right-hand side of the paper.

2. Use polyester fiberfill to apply crimson red ink to the three columns. Remove the masking tape.

3. To create the second color in the plaid pattern, place a vertical strip of low-tack masking tape ¾" from the left-hand side of the paper. Place a second strip of tape ¼" from the first strip of tape. Place a third strip of tape ½" from the right-hand side of the paper and a fourth strip of tape ¾" to the left of the third strip.

4. Apply true blue ink to the two columns. Remove the masking tape.

5. Repeat Steps 3–4 to create four vertical mustard yellow columns and one vertical pesto green column.

6. Create the horizontal lines in the same manner. Remove all pieces of masking tape.

7. Use archival paper glue to adhere the plaid paper to an 8½" x 11" paper. Glue the 4" x 5" piece of vellum paper to the upper-left area of the plaid paper. Use quick-drying craft glue to adhere the green ribbon across the page.

8. Cut the remaining 8½" x 11" paper to slightly larger than the photograph. Use archival paper glue to adhere the photograph onto the paper. Glue the photograph to the lower right of the page.

9. Tear sections of text from the vellum paper with text. Glue the text onto the page as desired. Use quick-drying craft glue to adhere the star to the lower corner of the photograph.

Colors of Autumn are an amazing sight...

The chrisp, fresh air, easy to breath...

And the leaves turning to red from green...

The Butterfly

Materials

- 8½" x 11" sheet of vellum paper
- 8½" x 11" sheet of white scrapbook paper
- Archival paper glue
- Butterfly pin
- Embossing heat tool
- Flower paper punch
- Inks in crimson red, mustard yellow, and sepia
- Low-tack masking tape
- Photographs (2)
- Polyester fiberfill
- Quick-drying craft glue
- Quilter's masking tape

Instructions

1. Use low-tack masking tape to create a ¼" border around the four edges of the 8½" x 11" paper.

2. Apply a strip of quilter's masking tape 1" from the top of the page. Repeat the process on the bottom and sides of the paper.

3. Use polyester fiberfill to apply crimson red ink to the center of the page. Apply mustard yellow ink to the 1" border of the scrapbook paper. Randomly apply sepia ink to the paper.

4. Lightly heat the tape with the embossing heat tool. Carefully remove all pieces of tape.

5. Use archival paper glue to adhere the photographs to the center of the page. Remove the pin section from the back of the butterfly. Use quick-drying craft glue to adhere the butterfly to the page. Punch out flowers from vellum paper and use archival paper glue to adhere them to the page.

Italy

Materials

- 4" x 5" piece of scrap paper
- 7" x 10" piece of white scrapbook paper
- 8½" x 11" sheet of white scrapbook paper
- 8½" x 11" sheets of black scrapbook paper (2)
- Archival paper glue
- Computer and printer, or marker
- Craft scissors
- Embossing heat tool
- Ink in cranberry
- Low-tack masking tape
- Photographs (4)
- Polyester fiberfill
- Ruler

Instructions

1. Tear a 1⅛" "U" shape from the 4" x 5" scrap paper to create a stone-like stencil.

2. Apply masking tape around the edges of the 7" x 10" paper to create a very narrow border.

3. Place the stone stencil on the upper-left corner of the paper. Use polyester fiberfill and cranberry ink to stencil the stone-like pattern onto this paper.

4. Lightly heat the tape with the embossing heat tool. Carefully remove all pieces of tape.

5. Glue the stenciled paper to an 8½" x 11" black paper.

6. Print the page title onto the 8½" x 11" white paper. Cut the title from the paper. Cut a piece from the remaining 8½" x 11" black paper to slightly larger than the title paper. Glue the title paper to the black paper. Repeat this process to add black borders to each photograph.

7. Glue the title paper and the photographs to the page.

Graphic Design

Materials

- 8½" x 11" sheet of black scrapbook paper
- 8½" x 11" sheets of white scrapbook paper (3)
- 12"-square sheet of white scrapbook paper
- Archival paper glue
- Clock rubber stamp
- Craft scissors
- Embossing heat tool
- Inks in banana yellow, carnation pink, cobalt blue, and true blue
- Quilter's masking tape
- Photograph
- Polyester fiberfill
- Ruler

Instructions

1. Use quilter's masking tape to create a 1"-square pattern on the 12"-square paper. Use polyester fiberfill to apply true blue ink to the entire paper. Randomly apply cobalt blue ink over the true blue ink. Lightly heat the tape with the embossing heat tool. Carefully remove all pieces of tape.

2. Apply banana yellow ink to an 8½" x 11" white paper. Use banana yellow ink to stamp the clock image randomly on the paper. Cut the paper into four different-sized rectangles. Cut four pieces from a second 8½" x 11" white paper to slightly larger than each rectangle.

Glue the rectangles to the pieces of white paper.

3. Apply horizontal strips of quilter's masking tape to create a striped pattern on the remaining 8½" x 11" white paper. Apply carnation pink ink over the exposed areas of the paper. Lightly heat the tape with the embossing heat tool. Carefully remove all pieces of tape. Cut out a 2½" circle from the striped paper.

4. Glue a yellow rectangle to the upper-left corner of the 8½" x 11" black paper. Glue the circle to the upper-left corner of the yellow rectangle.

5. Cut out a section with four blue squares from the blue paper, leaving a narrow white border around the

squares. Glue the squares over the yellow rectangle and pink striped circle. Place another yellow rectangle over the blue squares.

6. Cut out a section from the blue paper with six blue squares and glue it to the lower-right corner of the page. Glue the two remaining yellow rectangles over the blue squares. Glue the photograph to the center of the page.

7. Cut out three blue squares and glue them to the lower-left corner. Cut out two blue squares and glue them to the upper-right of the page.

Shabby Chic

Materials

- ¼" hole punch
- 2" x 10¼" piece of white scrapbook paper
- 5½" x 10" piece of white scrapbook paper
- 8½" x 11" sheet of white scrapbook paper
- 8½" x 11" sheets of black scrapbook paper (2)
- Archival paper glue
- Butterfly wings rubber stamp
- Craft scissors
- Heart-shaped gems
- Inks in carnation pink and meadow green
- Large semicircle rubber stamp
- Low-tack masking tape
- Photograph
- Polyester fiberfill
- Rosebud stencil
- Small semicircle rubber stamp
- Vine stencil

Instructions

1. Use low-tack masking tape to secure the rosebud stencil to the 5½" x 10" paper. Use polyester fiberfill to apply carnation pink ink over the stencil. Apply meadow green ink to the leaf areas of the stencil.

2. Use masking tape to secure the vine stencil to the 2" x 10¼" paper. Apply meadow green ink over the stencil.

3. Glue the vine-patterned paper to the left side of an 8½" x 11" black paper.

4. Cut two strips from the bottom of the rosebud-patterned paper. Glue the largest piece of rosebud-patterned paper to the upper-right area of the black paper. Glue the strips of rosebud-patterned paper below the largest piece, aligning the bottom strip with the bottom of the vine-patterned piece.

5. Cut the remaining 8½" x 11" black paper to slightly larger than the photograph. Glue the photograph to the black paper. Glue the matted photograph to the scrapbook page.

6. Stamp the semicircle images in carnation pink ink onto the 8½" x 11" white paper. Cut out the images and glue to excess black scrapbook paper. Cut out the images again, leaving a narrow black border. Glue the images to the page.

7. Use carnation pink ink to stamp four butterfly wings onto excess white scrapbook paper. Cut out the image and arrange the wings in the shape of a flower on the page. Apply carnation pink ink to a small area of the white paper. Punch out a circle and glue to the center of the flower.

8. Glue heart-shaped gems to the semicircles.

Butterfly Dream

Materials

- 11"-square piece of white scrapbook paper
- 12"-square sheet of white scrapbook paper
- 12"-square sheets of black scrapbook paper (2)
- 22-gauge copper wire
- Archival paper glue

- Bird sticker
- Clear embossing ink pen
- Craft scissors
- Detail embossing powder in gold
- Embossing heat tool
- Inks in clear embossing, crimson red, and sepia
- Ivy rubber stamp

- Large butterfly rubber stamp
- Photograph
- Polyester fiberfill
- Small butterfly rubber stamp
- Talc-free baby powder

Instructions

1. Cut a corner from the 12"-square white paper to 6" x 10". Use polyester fiberfill to apply crimson red ink to the paper. Apply sepia ink over the crimson ink. Dust the paper with talc-free baby powder.

2. Tap the large butterfly rubber stamp onto the clear embossing ink pad. Stamp the image onto the crimson-sepia paper. Continue stamping the butterfly onto the paper until the paper is completely covered.

3. Use the clear embossing pen to scribble lines between the butterflies. Sprinkle gold detail embossing powder over the entire paper. Shake off the excess powder. With the embossing heat tool, heat the embossing powder on the paper.

4. Apply crimson and sepia inks to excess white paper. Use crimson ink to stamp a random ivy image onto the paper. Dust the paper with talc-free baby powder.

5. Use clear embossing ink to stamp the small butterfly over the ivy paper. Sprinkle gold detail embossing powder over the entire paper. Shake off excess powder. With the embossing heat tool, heat the embossing powder on the paper. Cut three small squares from the paper.

6. Glue the 11"-square paper to a 12"-square black paper. Glue the large butterfly paper to the upper part of the white paper.

7. Cut the remaining 12"-square black paper to approximately ½" larger all around than the photograph. Glue the photograph to the black paper. Glue the matted photograph to the center of the large butterfly paper.

8. Cut a strip from excess black scrapbook paper. Glue the strip below the photograph, then glue the three small butterfly-embossed squares just below the photograph.

9. Cut three small squares from excess black scrapbook paper to fit inside the three butterfly-embossed squares. Glue these squares to the center of the butterfly-embossed squares.

10. Attach the bird sticker above the center butterfly-embossed square. Create an embellishment from wire. Glue the wire over the center square.

Batik

Materials

- 1" x 11" strips of white scrapbook paper (2)
- 8½" x 11" sheet of black scrapbook paper
- 8½" x 11" sheet of white scrapbook paper
- 11"-square piece of white scrapbook paper
- 12"-square sheet of black scrapbook paper
- 12"-square sheet of white scrapbook paper
- Archival paper glue
- Clear embossing ink pen
- Clear gel craft glue
- Computer and printer, or marker
- Craft scissors
- Embossing heat tool
- Embossing powder in clear
- Ink in meadow green
- Large photograph
- Small photographs (2)
- Polyester fiberfill
- White tags (2)

Instructions

1. Cut or tear a corner from the 12"-square white paper to 6" square. Use the clear embossing ink pen to draw triangles on the paper. Draw a swirl in the center of each triangle. Sprinkle the clear embossing powder over the paper. Shake off the excess powder. With the embossing heat tool, heat the embossing powder on the paper.

2. Use polyester fiberfill to apply the meadow green ink over the embossed paper. Rub a clean piece of polyester fiberfill over the paper to remove any excess ink. Cut the paper in half.

3. Use archival paper glue to adhere the 11"-square paper to the 12"-square black paper.

4. Apply meadow green ink to the 1" x 11" strips. Glue a strip approximately ½" from the top of the 11"-square paper. Glue the second strip approximately ½" from the bottom.

5. Glue one half of the batik paper to the upper-left side of the page. Glue the second batik half to the lower-right side of the page.

6. Cut the 8½" x 11" black paper to slightly larger than the large photograph. Glue the photograph to the black paper, then glue the piece to the center of the page.

7. Glue the two small photographs to the tags. Use clear gel craft glue to attach one tag to the upper-right corner of the page. Glue the second tag to the lower-left corner of the page.

8. Type text onto an 8½" x 11" sheet of white scrapbook paper. Cut out the letters and glue them to the lower right-corner of the page.

Cousins

Multicolored Batik

Materials

- 5½"-square piece of white scrapbook paper
- 6"-square piece of white scrapbook paper
- 11"-square piece of white scrapbook paper
- 12"-square sheet of white scrapbook paper
- Archival paper glue
- Clear embossing ink pen
- Embossing heat tool
- Embossing powder in clear
- Fabric leaves with wire stems (3)
- Inks in aqua, clear embossing, cobalt blue, and meadow green
- Leaf rubber stamp
- Photograph
- Polyester fiberfill
- White tags (3)

Instructions

1. Use clear embossing ink to randomly stamp the leaf image onto the 11"-square paper. Use the clear embossing ink pen to draw wavy lines between the leaves.

2. Sprinkle the clear embossing powder over the paper. Shake off the excess powder. Using the embossing heat tool, heat the embossing powder on the paper.

3. Use polyester fiberfill to apply the meadow green ink to the leaves. Apply the ink darker on some areas of each leaf.

4. Apply aqua ink to the background areas of the leaf-stamped paper. Randomly apply the cobalt blue ink over the aqua ink.

5. Glue the multicolored paper to the 12"-square paper.

6. Apply aqua ink to the 5½"-square paper. Glue the photograph to the paper.

7. Glue the matted photograph to the 6"-square paper, then center and glue the 6"-square paper to the multicolored paper.

8. Glue a fabric leaf onto each of the tags. Glue the tags to the lower-left corner of the photograph.

Tricolored Stripes

Materials

- 8" x 10½" piece of white scrapbook paper
- 8½" x 11" sheets of black scrapbook paper (2)
- Adhesive foam dots
- Archival paper glue
- Butterfly rubber stamp
- Inks in clear embossing, meadow green, mustard yellow, and vermilion
- Low-tack masking tape
- Number rubber stamp
- Pear rubber stamp
- Photographs (2)
- Pigment powder in bronze metallic
- Polyester fiberfill
- Postcard rubber stamp
- Soft-bristle craft brush
- Spray fixative
- Talc-free baby powder
- Text rubber stamp

Instructions

1. Use low-tack masking tape to create a narrow border around the four edges of the 8" x 10½" paper. Place two strips of tape across the paper, spacing them evenly.

2. Use polyester fiberfill to apply vermilion ink to the exposed area at the top of the masked paper. Apply mustard yellow ink to the center exposed area of the masked paper, then apply meadow green ink to the bottom exposed area of the masked paper.

3. Dust the paper with talc-free baby powder. Use clear embossing ink to randomly stamp the five images over all three sections of the paper. Dip the soft-bristle craft brush into the bronze metallic powder, then dust the stamped images with the powder. Remove the masking tape. Spray the paper with fixative.

4. Glue the tricolored stamped paper to an 8½" x 11" black paper.

5. Cut the remaining 8½" x 11" black paper to slightly larger than the photographs. Glue the photographs to the pieces of black paper. Glue a matted photograph to the right-hand side of the page. Use foam dots to attach the remaining matted photograph to the center of the page.

Spring Is in the Air

Materials

- ½" hole punch
- 8½" x 11" sheet of black scrapbook paper
- 8½" x 11" sheet of vellum paper
- 8½" x 11" sheet of white scrapbook paper
- 11"-square piece of white scrapbook paper
- 12"-square sheet of black scrapbook paper
- Adhesive foam dots
- Archival paper glue
- Clear embossing ink pen (optional)
- Computer and printer, or marker
- Craft scissors
- Embossing heat tool (optional)
- Embossing powder in gold (optional)
- Flower paper punch
- Flower rubber stamp
- Inks in carnation pink and clear embossing
- Low-tack masking tape
- Paintbrush
- Photograph
- Pigment powder in salmon pink metallic
- Polyester fiberfill
- Soft-bristle craft brush
- Talc-free baby powder

Instructions

1. Use low-tack masking tape to create a ⅛" border on the four sides of the 11"-square paper. Use polyester fiberfill to apply carnation pink ink to the paper. Dust the paper with talc-free baby powder.

2. Tap the flower rubber stamp on the clear embossing ink pad. Randomly stamp the flower image onto the carnation pink paper. Dip the soft-bristle craft brush into the salmon pink metallic powder. Dust the stamped flowers with the powder. Use a clean, dry paintbrush to remove excess powder. Remove the tape.

3. Punch six flowers and three ½" circles from the 8½" x 11" white paper. Apply carnation pink ink to three flowers. Glue each white flower to the back of each pink flower. Glue a white circle to the center of each pink flower.

4. Glue the salmon pink background paper to the 12"-square paper. Cut the 8½" x 11" black paper to slightly larger than the photograph. Glue the photograph to the black paper, then glue the matted photograph to the center of the salmon pink background paper.

5. Use foam dots to attach the three flowers to the lower-right corner of the page.

6. Type text onto the 8½" x 11" vellum paper. Dust the letters with the salmon pink metallic powder. If desired, trace one word with the clear embossing ink pen. Sprinkle the gold embossing powder over the embossing ink. Shake off the excess powder. With the embossing heat tool, heat the embossing powder on the paper.

7. Cut the text from the vellum paper. Glue the vellum text to the upper-left corner of the page.

Spring is in the Air

Tone-on-tone Embossing

Materials

- 8½" x 11" sheet of vellum paper
- 11"-square piece of white scrapbook paper
- 12"-square sheet of white scrapbook paper
- 12"-square sheets of black scrapbook paper (2)
- Architectural image rubber stamp
- Archival paper glue
- Bee rubber stamp
- Clear gel craft glue
- Computer and printer, or marker
- Craft scissors
- Detail embossing powder in gold
- Embossing heat tool
- Embossing powders in blue and clear
- Inks in clear embossing, cobalt blue, and true blue
- Photograph
- Polyester fiberfill
- Small letters, numbers, or text for domino embellishment (optional)
- Talc-free baby powder
- White domino

Instructions

1. Use polyester fiberfill to apply true blue ink to the 12"-square white paper. Randomly apply cobalt blue ink over the true blue ink. Dust the paper with talc-free baby powder.

2. Tap the bee rubber stamp onto the clear embossing ink pad. Stamp the image onto the blue ink-colored paper. Continue stamping the bee onto the paper until completely covered. Sprinkle the blue embossing powder over the entire paper. Shake off the excess powder. With the embossing heat tool, heat the embossing powder on the paper. Cut two long rectangles of equal size from the paper.

3. Use archival paper glue to adhere the 11"-square paper to a 12"-square black paper. Glue a bee-embossed rectangle to the upper area of the page, then glue the second rectangle to the lower area.

4. Cut the remaining 12"-square black paper to slightly larger than the photograph. Glue the photograph to the black paper, then glue the matted photograph to the center of the page.

5. Print text onto the vellum paper. Tear out the first part of the text, then glue to the upper-left corner of the page. Tear out the second part of the text, then glue to the lower-right corner of the page.

6. Use the clear embossing ink to stamp the architectural image onto excess vellum paper. Sprinkle the gold detail embossing powder over the entire paper. Shake off the excess powder. With the embossing heat tool, heat the embossing powder on the paper. Glue the paper to the white domino. Glue letters, numbers, or text onto the domino, if desired. Let the glue dry. Use clear gel craft glue to adhere the domino to the vellum text on the lower-right side of the page.

We are...

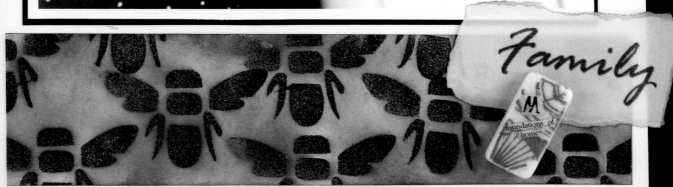

Family

foundations of home

A Day at the Zoo

A Day at the Zoo

Materials

- 5" x 7" piece of white scrapbook paper
- 7" x 8¾" piece of black scrapbook paper
- 8½"-square piece of white scrapbook paper
- 8½" x 11" sheet of vellum paper
- 9" x 10½" piece of white scrapbook paper
- 12"-square sheet of black scrapbook paper
- 22-gauge copper wire
- Archival paper glue
- Clear gel craft glue
- Computer and printer, or marker
- Detail embossing powder in gold
- Embossing heat tool
- Gold thread
- Inks in clear embossing and sepia
- Leaf rubber stamp
- Old earring
- Photograph
- Pigment powders in blue metallic and salmon pink metallic
- Polyester fiberfill
- Small white tag
- Soft-bristle craft brush
- Spray fixative
- Talc-free baby powder
- Text rubber stamp

Instructions

1. Use polyester fiberfill to apply sepia ink to the 8½"-square paper. Use the soft-bristle craft brush to randomly dust the salmon pink metallic powder over the sepia ink. Use the brush to dust the entire paper with talc-free baby powder.

2. Tap the leaf rubber stamp onto the clear embossing ink pad. Stamp the image onto the sepia paper until paper is completely covered. Sprinkle the gold detail embossing powder over the entire paper. Shake off the excess powder. Using the embossing heat tool, heat the embossing powder on the paper.

3. Apply sepia ink over the 5" x 7" paper. Use the sepia ink to randomly stamp the leaf image over the paper. Roll the paper to make a tube, then wrap the tube with copper wire.

4. Apply sepia ink to the small tag. Use the sepia ink to stamp the text image onto the tag.

5. Use copper wire to attach the small tag to the rolled-paper tube. Use clear gel craft glue to adhere the earring and gold thread to the rolled-paper tube.

6. Use archival paper glue to adhere the 9" x 10½" paper to the 12"-square black paper. Glue the leaf-embossed paper to the upper part of the white paper. Glue the 7" x 8¾" paper to the leaf-embossed paper. Glue the photograph to the upper part of the 7" x 8¾" paper.

7. Use clear gel craft glue to adhere the paper-tube embellishment below the photograph.

8. Type text onto the vellum paper. Dust the text with blue metallic powder. Spray the paper with fixative. Cut the text from the vellum. Use archival paper glue to adhere the text below the paper-tube embellishment.

Family

Green Leaves

Materials

- 6½" x 7½" piece of white scrapbook paper
- 8" x 10½" piece of white scrapbook paper
- 8½" x 11" sheet of vellum paper
- 8½" x 11" sheets of white scrapbook paper (2)
- Archival paper glue
- Clear embossing ink pen
- Clear gel craft glue
- Computer and printer, or marker
- Craft scissors
- Embossing heat tool
- Embossing powders in black and pesto green
- Fern rubber stamp
- Inks in clear embossing, meadow green, and pesto green
- Ivy stencil
- Lace scraps
- Large fabric leaves (2)
- Low-tack masking tape
- Oval tag
- Photograph
- Polyester fiberfill
- Small fabric leaf
- Talc-free baby powder
- Tiny paper flowers

Instructions

1. Use polyester fiberfill to lightly apply pesto ink to the 8" x 10½" paper. Dust paper with talc-free baby powder.

2. Tap the fern rubber stamp onto the clear embossing ink pad. Stamp the image onto the pesto green paper. Continue stamping the fern image onto the paper until the paper is completely covered. Sprinkle the pesto green embossing powder over the entire paper. Shake off the excess powder. With the embossing heat tool, heat the embossing powder on the paper.

3. Use low-tack masking tape to secure the ivy stencil to the 6½" x 7½" paper. Apply meadow green ink over the stencil. Remove the stencil from the paper.

4. Use clear gel craft glue to adhere the lace scraps to the oval tag. Glue the small fabric leaf to the tag. Glue the three paper flowers to the tag, covering the stem of the leaf.

5. Use archival paper glue to adhere the fern background paper to an 8 1/2" x 11" paper. Glue the ivy paper below the top edge of the fern paper.

6. Cut the remaining 8½" x 11" paper to slightly larger than the photograph. Use the clear embossing ink pen to fill in a ½" border around all four edges of the paper. Sprinkle the pesto green embossing powder over the entire paper. Shake off the excess powder. With the embossing heat tool, heat the embossing powder on the paper. Glue the photograph to the paper, then glue the matted photograph to the center of the ivy paper.

7. Print text onto the vellum paper. Dust the paper with talc-free baby powder. Trace the text with the clear embossing ink pen. Sprinkle the black embossing powder over the text. Shake off the excess powder. With the embossing heat tool, heat the embossing powder on the paper.

8. Cut the text from the vellum. Glue the vellum text above the right-hand side of the photograph.

9. Use clear gel craft glue to adhere the large fabric leaves and the oval tag above the photograph.

Torn-edged Pink Metallic

Materials

- 8½" x 11" sheets of white scrapbook paper (2)
- Alphabet stencil
- Archival paper glue
- Computer and printer, or marker
- Craft scissors
- Inks in carnation pink and clear embossing
- Little hands rubber stamp
- Low-tack masking tape
- Paintbrush
- Photographs (4–5)
- Pigment powder in salmon pink metallic
- Polyester fiberfill
- Soft-bristle craft brush
- Spray fixative
- Talc-free baby powder

Instructions

1. Tear two long strips of low-tack masking tape in half lengthwise. Place the torn tape on the four edges of an 8½" x 11" paper to create a border. Use polyester fiberfill to apply carnation pink ink to the paper. Dust the paper with talc-free baby powder.

2. Tap the little hands rubber stamp on the clear embossing ink pad. Randomly stamp the hands image over the carnation pink paper. Dip the soft-bristle craft brush into the salmon pink metallic powder, then dust the stamped hands with the powder. Use a clean, dry paintbrush to remove the excess powder. Spray the paper with fixative.

3. Use masking tape to secure the alphabet stencil to the carnation pink paper. Apply carnation pink ink over the stencil. Dust the salmon pink metallic powder over the stencil. Remove the stencil from the paper. Remove the tape.

4. Print text onto the remaining 8½" x 11" paper. Cut the text from the paper. Glue the text to the upper part of the page.

5. Glue photographs as desired below the text.

Baking Bread
with Grandma March

Stamped Embellishments

Materials

- 8½" x 11" sheet of black scrapbook paper
- 8½" x 11" sheets of white scrapbook paper (2)
- Adhesive foam dots
- Archival paper glue
- Clear gel craft glue
- Craft scissors
- Detail embossing powder in black
- Embossing heat tool
- Faux pearls
- Floral rubber stamp
- Inks in banana yellow, carnation pink, clear embossing, meadow green, and purple
- Low-tack masking tape
- Paper rose
- Photograph
- Polyester fiberfill
- Talc-free baby powder
- White domino
- White tulle

Instructions

1. Use low-tack masking tape to create a ¼" border on the four sides of an 8½" x 11" white paper. Use polyester fiberfill to apply purple ink to the paper. Remove the tape.

2. Cut three squares from the remaining 8½" x 11" white paper. Dust the paper with talc-free baby powder. Tap the floral rubber stamp onto the clear embossing ink pad. Stamp the image on the squares. Sprinkle the black detail embossing powder on the stamped image. Shake off the excess powder. With the embossing heat tool, heat the embossing powder on the paper.

3. Apply carnation pink ink to the flowers, meadow green to the leaves, and banana yellow to the background areas.

4. Tie white tulle around the domino. Cut off excess tulle. Use clear gel craft glue to adhere the faux pearls below the tulle on the right-hand side of the domino. Use archival paper glue to adhere the paper rose above the tulle knot.

5. Glue one floral-embossed square to the upper-left corner of the purple background paper. Glue the second square to the right-hand side of the paper. Tilt the last square to create a diamond shape. Glue it to the lower-left side of the purple paper.

6. Cut a corner from the 8½" x 11" black paper to slightly larger than the photograph. Glue photograph to the black paper. Use foam dots to attach the matted photograph over the purple paper.

7. Use clear gel craft glue to adhere the domino above the embossed floral diamond.

Bronze-aged Art

Materials

- 8" x 10½" piece of white scrapbook paper
- 8½" x 11" sheets of black scrapbook paper (2)
- Adhesive foam dots
- Archival paper glue
- Caveman hands rubber stamp
- Clear gel craft glue
- Craft scissors
- Fabric leaf
- Faux pearls
- Inks in clear embossing, mustard yellow, true blue, and vermilion
- Oval tag
- Paintbrush
- Paper flower
- Photograph
- Pigment powder in bronze metallic
- Polyester fiberfill
- Primitive deer rubber stamp
- Primitive horse rubber stamp
- Quick-drying craft glue
- Quilter's masking tape
- Silver heart charm
- Spray fixative
- Talc-free baby powder
- White lace

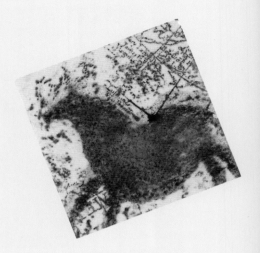

Instructions

1. Use quilter's masking tape to create a grid with nine squares on the 8" x 10½" paper. Use polyester fiberfill to apply mustard yellow, true blue, and vermilion inks to the squares. Dust the paper with talc-free baby powder.

2. Use clear embossing ink to stamp the primitive deer, primitive horse, and caveman hands in the colored squares. Dust the images with bronze metallic powder. Use a clean, dry paintbrush to remove excess powder. Carefully remove the quilter's masking tape. Spray the paper with fixative.

3. Use foam dots to attach the fabric leaf to the oval tag. Use clear gel craft glue to adhere the faux pearls in the center of the leaf. Use a dimensional foam dot to attach the silver heart charm below the fabric leaf. Use archival paper glue to adhere the paper flower above the silver heart charm.

4. Glue the bronzed squares paper to a sheet of black scrapbook paper. Use quick-drying craft glue to adhere the lace to the left-hand side of the bronzed squares paper.

5. Cut the remaining 8½" x 11" black paper to slightly larger than the photograph. Glue the photograph to the paper. Use foam dots to attach the matted photograph to the center of the page.

6. Use clear gel craft glue to adhere the oval embellishment to the upper-left side of the page.

If Wishes Came True

Materials

- ½" hole punch
- 8½" x 11" sheet of black scrapbook paper
- 8½" x 11" sheets of white scrapbook paper (3)
- 10½"-square piece of white scrapbook paper
- 12"-square sheet of black scrapbook paper
- Adhesive foam dots
- Archival paper glue
- Clear gel craft glue
- Computer and printer, or marker
- Craft scissors
- Fabric leaves (3)
- Inks in banana yellow, orange, pesto green, and true blue
- Low-tack masking tape
- Oval tag
- Photographs (4)
- Polyester fiberfill
- Silver heart charm
- White thread

Instructions

1. Use low-tack masking tape to create a narrow border on the 10½" square paper.

2. Cut a "grass blades" stencil from an 8½" x 11" white paper. Set aside the cut-out area of the stencil. *Note: You will use this as an embellishment on the scrapbook page later.* Use polyester fiberfill to apply pesto green ink over the stencil repeatedly onto the 10½"-square paper. Apply true blue ink to the top of the paper to simulate sky. Remove the tape.

3. Cut three different-sized rectangles from a second 8½" x 11" white paper. Apply banana yellow ink to the two smaller rectangles. Apply orange ink to the edges of these rectangles.

4. Apply banana yellow ink to the right-hand half of the larger rectangle. Apply orange ink to the yellow edges. Apply true blue ink to the remaining parts of the same rectangle. Apply pesto green ink to the blue edges.

5. Use archival paper glue to adhere the stenciled paper to the 12"-square black paper. Glue a yellow rectangle to the left-hand side of the stenciled paper. Glue the remaining yellow rectangle to the right-hand side of the stenciled paper. Glue the fabric leaves over the right-hand rectangle.

6. Cut an 8½" x 11" black paper to slightly larger than each of the photographs. Glue the photographs to the pieces of black paper. Center and glue the main matted photograph to the grass background paper. Glue the remaining matted photographs to the grass background paper as desired.

7. Apply pesto green ink to the cut-out area of the grass blades stencil. Glue the grass blades to the left-hand side of the page. Glue the yellow and blue rectangle below the main photograph.

8. Print "Smile" and "If wishes came true, I'd be at the Zoo!" onto the remaining 8½" x 11" white paper.

Note: Make sure to print "Smile" so that each letter can be punched out into ½" circles. Use the ½" hole punch to cut out each letter of the word "Smile." Use foam dots to attach the letters to the left-hand side of the left yellow rectangle.

9. Cut the remaining text from the paper. Apply banana yellow ink over the text. Cut an excess piece of black scrapbook paper to slightly larger than the text and using the archival paper glue, adhere the text to the black paper. Glue the matted text to the lower-right side of the blue and yellow rectangle.

10. Wrap thread around each of the "Smile" letters. Glue the ends of the threads to the lower-left corner of the yellow text paper. Glue an oval tag over the thread ends to cover them.

11. Use clear gel craft glue to adhere a silver heart charm to the face of the tag.

S
M
I
L
E

If wishes came true,
I'd be at the Zoo!

Pink Patchwork

Materials

- 1" circle stencil
- 8½" x 11" sheet of vellum paper
- 8½" x 11" sheet of white scrapbook paper
- 11½"-square piece of white scrapbook paper
- 12"-square sheets of white scrapbook paper (2)
- Alphabet stencil
- Archival paper glue
- Computer and printer, or marker
- Craft scissors
- Floral stencil
- Heart paper punch
- Inks in carnation pink and crimson red
- Large photograph
- Polyester fiberfill
- Ruler
- Small photograph

Instructions

1. Use polyester fiberfill to apply carnation pink ink over the 11½"-square paper. Apply crimson red ink over the carnation pink ink.

2. Cut an 8½" x 11" white paper in half. Apply a light coat of crimson red ink over one half. Cover the inked paper with the floral stencil. Apply crimson red ink over the stencil. Remove the stencil from the paper. Cut a rectangle from this paper.

3. Apply a light coat of crimson red ink over the remaining half of the paper. Cover the paper with the circle stencil. Apply crimson red ink over the stencil. Remove the circle stencil. Use an alphabet stencil to apply one letter to each circle. Remove the alphabet stencil. Cut a rectangle from this paper to approximately 4" x 6".

4. Glue the pink paper to a 12"-square white paper. Cut a ¼" x 12" strip of paper from the remaining 12"-square white paper. Apply carnation pink ink to this paper. Glue the strip across the center of the pink background paper.

5. Glue the floral stencil rectangle to the right of the page, just below the carnation pink strip. Glue the circle and alphabet rectangle to the lower left of the page.

6. Glue the large photograph to the pink background paper. Glue the small photograph near the lower-left side of the large photograph.

7. Type text onto the vellum paper. Cut out the text and glue it to the scrapbook page.

8. Punch out eight hearts from excess white scrapbook paper. Apply carnation pink ink to the hearts. Glue the hearts to the page.

Family

Meg
Katie

Dad
Boots
Paul
Brian

Family

Mother and Son

Materials

- ⅛" hole punch
- 8½" x 11" sheet of white scrapbook paper
- 10"-square piece of white scrapbook paper
- 12"-square sheet of black scrapbook paper
- Adhesive foam dots
- Archival paper glue
- Computer and printer, or marker
- Coral heart
- Craft scissors
- Inks in black and gray
- Oval photograph
- Pencil
- Polyester fiberfill
- Silver heart charms (2)
- White thread

Instructions

1. Place the oval photograph in the center of the 10"-square paper. Lightly outline the photograph in pencil. Remove the photograph. *Note: You will use this outline as a guide for where to apply inks.*

2. Use polyester fiberfill to lightly apply gray ink around the outline on the paper. Lightly apply black ink over the gray ink.

3. Glue the gray background paper to the 12"-square paper. Punch a small hole on each side of the photograph. Tie the silver heart charms to the photograph with white thread.

4. Punch a hole in the bottom of the photograph. Tie the coral heart to the bottom of the photograph with white thread.

5. Use foam dots to attach the photograph to the gray background paper. Print text onto the 8½" x 11" paper. Cut out the text and glue it to the bottom of the scrapbook page.

Night Fairy

Materials

- 8" x 10½" piece of white scrapbook paper
- 8½" x 11" sheet of black scrapbook paper
- 8½" x 11" sheet of white scrapbook paper
- Adhesive foam dots
- Archival paper glue
- Embossed wallpaper, or other embossed paper
- Faux pearls
- Flower paper punch
- Green eyelash ribbon
- Inks in banana yellow, carnation pink, cobalt blue, Prussian blue, and true blue
- Large photograph
- Moon paper punch
- Polyester fiberfill
- Quick-drying craft glue
- Star paper punch

Instructions

1. Use polyester fiberfill to randomly apply true blue ink over the 8" x 10½" paper. Apply cobalt blue ink randomly over the true blue ink. Apply Prussian blue ink to the edges of the paper.

2. Use archival paper glue to adhere the blue paper to the black scrapbook paper. Punch several stars and a moon from the 8½" x 11" white paper. Color the moon and some stars with yellow ink. Glue the stars and moon to the blue paper.

3. Cut out a figure from the photograph. Cut out images from embossed wallpaper. Glue the wallpaper cutouts to the back of the photograph to simulate wings. Use foam dots to attach the photograph to the blue paper.

4. Use quick-drying craft glue to adhere the green eyelash ribbon over the figure to create a sash.

5. Apply carnation pink ink to excess white scrapbook paper. Punch several flowers from the inked paper. Glue the flowers around the green eyelash ribbon. Glue faux pearls onto the green eyelash ribbon.

My Backyard
Mary Ann Gifford
Big blue birds babbling by,
Dew on the grass standing ever so high,
Flowers that dance show a beautiful sight,
As the sun shines an iridescent glow like a flashlight,
The scent of fresh air is an ocean that makes me glad,
That I can revisit the backyard I once had.

Starry Night

Materials

- 8½" x 11" sheet of vellum paper
- 8½" x 11" sheet of white scrapbook paper
- 11"-square piece of white scrapbook paper
- 12"-square sheet of black scrapbook paper
- Adhesive foam dots
- Archival paper glue
- Clear gel craft glue
- Computer and printer, or marker
- Craft scissors
- Embossing heat tool
- Embossing powder in clear
- Faux pearls
- Gold jump ring
- Inks in clear embossing and true blue
- Large star rubber stamp
- Photograph
- Polyester fiberfill
- Ruler
- Small star rubber stamp
- White tulle (4")

Instructions

1. Use clear embossing ink to stamp large and small stars onto the 11"-square paper. Sprinkle embossing powder over the entire paper. Shake off the excess powder. With the embossing heat tool, heat the embossing powder on the paper. Use polyester fiberfill to apply true blue ink over the embossed images.

2. Cut the star background paper in half diagonally, cutting around stars. Use archival paper glue to adhere the star paper to the 12"-square paper.

3. Cut out an image from the photograph. Thread the white tulle through the gold jump ring. Use clear gel craft glue to adhere the jump ring to the center of the image. Glue the ends of the tulle behind the image. Glue the faux pearls onto the image. Use foam dots to attach the image to the star paper.

4. Print a poem onto the vellum paper. Cut the poem from the paper. Cut a corner from the 8½" x 11" white paper to slightly smaller than the vellum paper. Use archival paper glue to adhere the vellum paper over the white paper. Glue the poem piece to the upper-right side of the star paper.

5. Cut a ⅛" x 4" strip from excess white scrapbook paper. Glue the strip to the left-hand side of the page. Cut a ⅛" x 1" strip from white scrapbook paper. Glue the strip to the lower-right side of the page. Cut a ⅛" x 4½" strip from white scrapbook paper. Apply true blue ink over the strip. Glue the strip to the lower area of the page.

6. Cut out stars from the remaining star background paper. Glue the stars as desired to the page.

Moon Dance

Materials

- ¼" hole punch
- 8½" x 10" piece of white scrapbook paper
- 8½" x 11" sheet of vellum paper
- 12"-square sheets of white scrapbook paper (2)
- Adhesive foam dots
- Alphabet rubber stamps
- Archival paper glue
- Butterfly wing rubber stamp
- Crackle rubber stamp
- Craft scissors
- Gold metallic pigment powder
- Gold thread
- Inks in banana yellow, black, crimson red, meadow green, orange, Prussian blue, and true blue
- Ivy rubber stamp
- Leaf paper punch
- Photograph
- Polyester fiberfill
- Star rubber stamp
- White scrap paper
- White tags (5)

Instructions

1. Use polyester fiberfill to apply meadow green ink to the 8½" x 10" paper. Apply Prussian blue ink to the edges of the paper. Use meadow green ink to stamp the ivy image over the paper.

2. Place five white tags next to each other. Tear a piece from white scrap paper and place the torn edge near the top of all five tags. Apply true blue ink onto the exposed areas of the tags. Move the scrap paper down the tag. Apply true blue ink to the exposed areas of the tags. Repeat the process until the entire tag is colored. Use black ink to stamp the word "Dance" on the tags.

3. Glue the green background paper horizontally to a 12"-square paper. Cut a 7" wedge shape from the remaining 12"-square paper. Apply banana yellow ink over the wedge. Use orange ink to stamp the ivy pattern over the wedge. Glue the wedge to the lower-right side of the green background paper.

4. Cut out a moon shape from excess white scrapbook paper. Apply banana yellow ink over the moon shape. Use the orange ink to stamp the crackle image over the moon. Glue the moon to the center of the green background paper.

5. Punch several leaves from excess white scrapbook paper. Apply crimson red ink to two-thirds of the leaves and meadow green ink to one-third. Cut strips for stems from excess white scrapbook paper and apply meadow green ink to the stems. Punch out circles for flower centers and apply banana yellow ink to the circles.

6. Glue the stems to the left-hand side of the scrapbook page. Glue five crimson red ink leaves together to form a flower. Glue a yellow circle in the center of each flower. Repeat this process to create as many flowers as desired on the scrapbook page. Glue the green leaves to the stems.

7. Cut a figure from the photograph.

8. Apply banana yellow and orange ink to the vellum paper. Using black ink, stamp two butterfly wings on the paper. Dust the wings with gold metallic powder. Cut out each wing and glue the wings to the back of the figure. Use foam dots to attach the figure over the moon on the page.

9. Stamp five yellow stars onto excess white scrapbook paper. Cut out the stars and use foam dots to attach them to the right-hand side of the scrapbook page.

10. Use foam dots to arrange the tags on the bottom of the scrapbook page. Use gold thread to tie each tag to the moon.

Three Muses

Materials

- 8½" x 11" sheet of black scrapbook paper
- 8½" x 11" sheets of white scrapbook paper (2)
- 10½"-square piece of white scrapbook paper
- 12"-square sheet of black scrapbook paper
- 12"-square sheet of white scrapbook paper
- Architectural image rubber stamp
- Archival paper glue
- Computer and printer, or marker
- Craft scissors
- Heart paper punch
- Heart rubber stamp
- Inks in banana yellow, black, crimson red, meadow green, and true blue
- Oval tag
- Photographs (3)
- Playing cards
- Polyester fiberfill
- Printed poem
- Ruler
- Scraps of lace
- Square tag
- White rectangular tag

Instructions

1. Cut three rectangles from an 8½" x 11" white paper. Use polyester fiber-fill to apply crimson red ink over each of the rectangles. Stamp the heart images with crimson red ink onto the crimson rectangles.

2. Cut a 4" square from excess white scrapbook paper. Randomly apply banana yellow, crimson red, and true blue inks to the square. Use black ink to stamp the architectural image over the paper. Cut the paper to fit inside the rectangular, square, and oval tags. Glue small bits of lace onto the tags.

3. Attach the collage tags to the red rectangles. Cut out lines from the printed poem and glue the lines onto the red rectangles.

4. Cut three small rectangles from excess white scrapbook paper. Apply banana yellow ink to the rectangles. Glue a rectangle to the upper area of each red background base. Glue a photograph over each yellow rectangle. Cut out a number and diamond from three playing cards. Glue them on the red rectangles.

5. Cut out wing shapes from the 8½" x 11" black paper. Glue the wings to the back of the red rectangles.

6. Glue the 10½"-square paper to the 12"-square black paper.

7. Tear a strip from the 12"-square white paper. Trim the strip to 10½" long. Apply meadow green ink to the strip. Glue the strip to the bottom of the 10½"-square paper.

8. Print text onto the remaining 8½" x 11" white paper. Cut out the text and glue it just above the meadow green paper.

9. Glue the rectangles to the page.

10. Punch ten hearts from excess white scrapbook paper. Apply true blue ink to each heart. Glue two hearts below each rectangle. Glue additional hearts near the photographs.

Three Muses

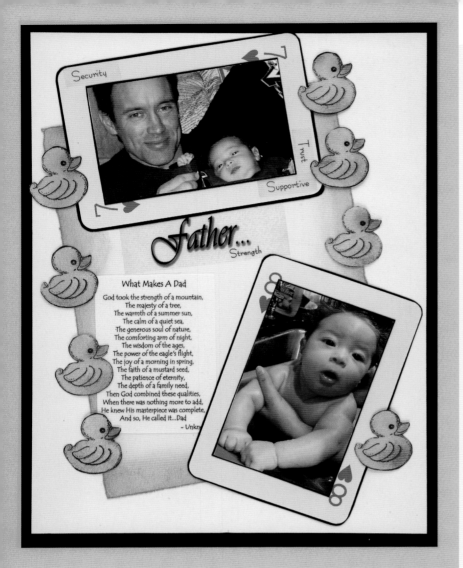

Playing Cards

Materials

- 2½" x 4" pieces of black scrapbook paper (2)
- 6" x 8" piece of white scrapbook paper
- 8" x 10" piece of white scrapbook paper
- 8½" x 11" sheet of black scrapbook paper
- 8½" x 11" sheet of white scrapbook paper
- Archival paper glue
- Craft scissors
- Inks in banana yellow, black, and orange
- Photographs (2)
- Playing cards (2)
- Polyester fiberfill
- Rubber duck rubber stamp
- Text stickers

Instructions

1. Cut the photographs to slightly smaller than the 2½" x 4" papers. Glue the photographs to the papers. Glue each matted photograph to the face of a playing card. Apply text stickers to the face of each playing card.

2. Glue the 8" x 10" paper to the 8½" x 11" black paper.

3. Use polyester fiberfill to apply banana yellow ink to the edges of the 6" x 8" paper. Apply orange ink over the banana yellow ink. Glue this paper at a slant to the 8" x 10" paper.

4. Glue a photograph playing card to the top of the page. Glue the remaining card to the bottom of the page. Attach more text stickers as desired to the page.

5. Use black ink to stamp eight rubber ducks on the 8½" x 11" white paper. Apply banana yellow and orange ink to the rubber ducks. Cut out the rubber ducks and glue them to the page.

Imagination

Materials

- ⅛" x 6" white ribbon
- 6" x 9" white tulle
- 8½" x 11" sheets of black scrapbook paper (2)
- 8½" x 11" sheets of white scrapbook paper (3)
- Archival paper glue
- Craft scissors
- Flower paper punch
- Inks in carnation pink, meadow green, and true blue
- Leaf paper punch
- Photograph
- Polyester fiberfill
- Ruler
- Star paper punch

Instructions

1. Cut a heart shape from an 8½" x 11" white paper to create a heart stencil. Use polyester fiberfill to apply true blue ink to the stencil repeatedly onto a second 8½" x 11" white paper. Cut the paper to 6½" x 8". Glue the blue heart paper onto the remaining 8½" x 11" white paper. Trim the white paper to slightly larger than the blue heart paper.

2. Glue the heart paper to the center of the 8½" x 11" black paper.

3. Punch out nine stars and eight flowers from excess white scrapbook paper. Glue seven stars on the black paper. Glue two stars on the blue background.

4. Tie white ribbon around one end of the tulle. Glue this end of the tulle to the upper-left corner of the page. Glue the other end of the tulle to the back of the page. Glue the remaining 8½" x 11" black paper to the back of the page.

5. Cut a figure from the photograph. Glue the figure to the bottom of the heart paper. Glue the eight white flowers diagonally over the heart paper.

6. Punch out five leaves and apply meadow green ink to the leaves. Glue the leaves below the image. Punch out several flowers and apply carnation pink ink to the flowers. Glue the pink flowers below the photograph.

Geometric Design

Materials

- ¼" x 3" strip of white scrapbook paper with torn edges
- 2" x 4" piece of white scrapbook paper
- 4"-square pieces of white scrapbook paper (2)
- 5" x 7" piece of black scrapbook paper
- 8" x 10½" piece of white scrapbook paper
- 8½" x 11" sheet of black scrapbook paper
- 8½" x 11" sheets of white scrapbook paper (2)
- Acrylic paint in gold
- Archival paper glue
- Clear gel craft glue
- Craft scissors
- Decorative-edged scissors
- Flower button
- Inks in cobalt blue, crimson red, Prussian blue, sepia, and true blue
- Paintbrush
- Photograph
- Polyester fiberfill
- Round button
- Scrap paper with torn edges
- Swirl rubber stamp
- Tiny diamond rubber stamp

Instructions

1. Use polyester fiberfill to apply crimson red ink to a 4"-square paper. Place the torn scrap paper vertically on the right-hand side of the 4" square. Apply crimson red ink over the edges of the stencil and on the 4" square. Move the stencil to the left and repeat the process until the entire page is covered.

2. Use crimson red ink to stamp the swirl image over the square. Use gold acrylic paint to stamp three swirls.

3. Cut a piece from an 8½" x 11" white paper to slightly larger than the red swirl paper. Use archival paper glue to adhere the red swirl paper to the white paper.

4. Apply Prussian blue ink to the remaining 4"-square paper. Place the torn paper vertically on the right-hand side of the square. Apply cobalt ink over the edges of the stencil and onto the square. Move the stencil to the left and repeat the process until the entire page is covered.

5. Use Prussian blue ink to stamp the swirl image over the blue paper. Use gold acrylic paint to stamp swirls over the paper. Tear the blue swirl embellishment paper in half. Place one half diagonally on the left-hand side of the 2" x 4" paper. Place the remaining half diagonally on the right-hand side of the 2" x 4" paper.

6. Apply crimson red ink to the ¼" x 3" paper. Glue the crimson red paper to the center of the 2" x 4" paper. Cut a corner from the remaining 8½" x 11" white paper to slightly larger than the blue swirl embellishment paper and glue it to the back of the paper.

7. Draw a 4" circle on excess white scrapbook paper. Apply cobalt blue ink to the circle. Use cobalt blue ink to stamp the diamond pattern onto the circle. Use decorative-edged scissors to cut out the circle. Use craft scissors to cut the circle into four wedges. Cut excess white scrapbook paper to slightly larger than one wedge. Apply Prussian blue ink to the white wedge. Glue the cobalt wedge to the Prussian blue wedge.

8. Randomly apply sepia ink to the 8" x 10½" paper. Glue the sepia paper the 8½" x 11" black paper.

9. Glue the red swirl paper to the upper-left corner of the sepia paper.

10. Glue the 5" x 7" paper to the center of the sepia paper. Glue the photograph to the upper-left corner of the 5" x 7" paper. Glue the blue swirl paper below the 5" x 7" paper.

11. Glue the wedge embellishment over the blue swirl paper. Cut a small rectangle from excess white scrapbook paper and paint it with gold. Glue the gold rectangle over the wedge embellishment. Use clear gel craft glue to adhere the round button onto the flower button. Glue the buttons to the top of the gold rectangle.

Emma Rose

Materials

- 2½" x 3½" piece of white watercolor paper
- 8" x 10½" piece of white scrapbook paper
- 8¼" x 10¾" piece of white scrapbook paper
- 8½" x 11" sheet of black scrapbook paper
- 8½" x 11" sheet of white scrapbook paper
- Archival paper glue
- Butterfly rubber stamp
- Computer and printer, or marker
- Craft scissors
- Cream flowers (3)
- Detail embossing powder in silver
- Embossing heat tool
- Flower rubber stamp
- Inks in carnation pink, clear embossing, meadow green, purple, and true blue
- Large photograph
- Pink buttons (3)
- Polyester fiberfill
- Quick-drying craft glue
- Quilter's masking tape
- Small photograph
- Wide fabric trim (3½")

Instructions

1. Use carnation pink ink to stamp the flower image onto the 8" x 10½" paper. Repeat the process until the entire paper is covered. Cut off the top part of the paper, using the shape of the stamped flowers as a guide.

2. Place four strips of quilter's masking tape vertically on the 2½" x 3½" paper. Use polyester fiberfill to apply carnation pink ink to the watercolor paper. Carefully remove the quilter's masking tape.

3. Use quick-drying craft glue to adhere the fabric trim to the top edge of the watercolor paper. Glue the buttons over the fabric trim.

4. Use archival paper glue to adhere the pink flower paper to the 8¼" x 10¾" paper. Glue this paper to the black scrapbook paper.

5. Cut out an image from the large photograph. Glue the image over the pink flower paper.

6. Print text onto the 8½" x 11" white paper. Cut the text from the paper. Glue text to the pink stripe embellishment. Glue the pink stripe embellishment over the lower-right corner of the page.

7. Use clear embossing ink to stamp two butterflies onto excess white scrapbook paper. Sprinkle the silver detail embossing powder over the entire paper. Shake off the excess powder. With the embossing heat tool, heat the embossing powder on the paper.

8. Apply meadow green, true blue, and purple inks to the butterflies as desired. Glue one butterfly to the upper right of the page. Glue the remaining butterfly to the lower left of the page.

9. Cut a wavy strip from excess pink flower background paper. Glue the strip to the upper part of the page. Glue three flowers over the strip.

10. Cut a piece from excess white scrapbook paper to slightly larger than the small photograph. Glue the photograph to the paper. Glue the matted photograph just above the pink striped embellishment.

Emma Rose came into our life on a warm Sunday afternoon. Hearing a knock on the door, Paul opened it to find a wide-eyed kind soul. "Did you loose a kitten." she asked. "No," replied Paul. "I don't know what to do!" continued the kind soul, "I am allergic to cats and this poor little kitten is lost, she is too young to survive on her own!"

With that, *Emma Rose* came into our life.

Vintage Projects

Lace Edge

Materials

- ½" hole punch
- 6"-square piece of white scrapbook paper
- 8½" x 11" sheet of black scrapbook paper
- 8½" x 11" sheet of white scrapbook paper
- 11"-square piece of white scrapbook paper
- 12"-square sheet of black scrapbook paper
- Archival paper glue
- Computer and printer, or marker
- Inks in carnation pink and sepia
- Low-tack masking tape
- Photograph
- Polyester fiberfill
- White embossed wallpaper

Instructions

1. Use low-tack masking tape to create a ½" border around the four edges of the 11"-square paper. Place a piece of low-tack masking tape ⅛" from the bottom of the taped border. Place a second piece of tape ⅛" up from the previous piece of masking tape.

2. Use polyester fiberfill to apply carnation pink ink to the exposed areas of the paper. Remove the two pieces of low-tack masking tape from the bottom of the paper.

3. Cut shapes from the embossed wallpaper. Glue the shapes to the left- and right-hand sides of the carnation pink paper, matching the edges with the edges of the masking tape. Apply carnation pink ink over the embossed shapes. Lightly apply sepia ink over the embossed shapes.

4. Remove the masking tape from the edges of the pink paper. Glue the pink paper to the 12"-square paper.

5. Apply the carnation pink ink to the 6"-square paper. Punch 14 circles from the paper. Glue ten circles to the bottom of the pink paper.

6. Glue four circles to the upper-right side of the pink paper. Place a piece of low-tack masking tape ½" to the left of the four circles. Apply carnation pink ink above the left-hand edge of the masking tape. Remove the tape.

7. Cut the 8½" x 11" black paper to slightly larger than the photograph. Glue the photograph to the black paper. Glue the matted photograph to the page.

8. Print text onto the 8½" x 11" white paper. Cut the text from the paper. Glue the text to the bottom of the page.

JULIANA FIEHL-PETRONE

Family of Salvatore Lopetrone

Theresa Lopetrone-Naples

Josephine, Barbara, Anthony
Sam, Carmen, Mary Josephine

Anthony Lopetrone

Ivy Corner

Materials

- 8½" x 11" sheet of white scrapbook paper
- 11"-square piece of white scrapbook paper
- 12"-square sheet of black scrapbook paper
- Archival paper glue
- Computer and printer or marker
- Craft scissors
- Inks in carnation pink, pesto green, and sepia
- Ivy stencil
- Low-tack masking tape
- Photographs (3)
- Polyester fiberfill

Instructions

1. Use low-tack masking tape to create a ½" border around the four edges of the 11"-square paper. Use polyester fiberfill to apply pesto green ink to the left-hand side and bottom of the paper.

2. Use low-tack masking tape to secure the ivy stencil along the left-hand side of the paper. Apply meadow green ink over the stencil. Remove the stencil. Place the stencil along the bottom of the paper. Apply meadow green ink over the stencil. Remove the stencil.

3. Lightly apply carnation pink ink over the white areas of the paper. Apply sepia ink to all four sides of the paper. Remove the tape.

4. Glue the ivy corner paper to the 12"-square paper.

5. Type the page title onto the 8½" x 11" paper. Cut the title from the paper. Glue the title to the top of the page.

6. Glue the photographs to the page as desired.

Pink Pears

Materials

- 8½" x 11" sheets of white scrapbook paper (2)
- Archival paper glue
- Craft scissors
- Flower paper punch
- Inks in carnation pink and sepia
- Low-tack masking tape
- Pear rubber stamp
- Photograph
- Pink paper roses
- Polyester fiberfill

Instructions

1. Use low-tack masking tape to create a ½" border around the four edges of an 8½" x 11" white paper. Use polyester fiberfill to apply carnation pink ink to the paper.

2. Using carnation pink ink, randomly stamp the pear image onto the paper. Apply sepia ink over the paper. Carefully remove the masking tape from the paper.

3. Cut the remaining 8½" x 11" white paper to slightly larger than the photograph. Glue the photograph to the paper. Glue the matted photograph to the center of the carnation pink paper.

4. Punch four flowers from excess white scrapbook paper. Glue two flowers above the photograph and two flowers below the photograph.

5. Glue the pink paper roses to the center of each flower.

War Hero

Materials

- 8½" x 11" sheet of black scrapbook paper
- 8½" x 11" sheet of white scrapbook paper
- 10½" x 11" piece of white scrapbook paper
- 12"-square sheet of black scrapbook paper
- Adhesive foam dots
- Archival paper glue
- Computer and printer, or marker
- Craft scissors
- Inks in old-photograph brown, pesto green, and sepia
- Low-tack masking tape
- Military medal photocopies
- Photographs (4), one to fit the center of the large playing card
- Playing card
- Polyester fiberfill

Instructions

1. Use low-tack masking tape to create a ½" border around the four edges of the 10½" x 11" paper. Place a piece of low-tack masking tape diagonally across the page, from the upper-right corner to the lower-left corner.

2. Use polyester fiberfill to apply sepia ink to the right-hand side of the paper. Remove the diagonal tape. Apply a new piece of low-tack masking tape over sepia-colored paper to protect it from the pesto ink, then apply the pesto ink over the left-hand side of the paper. Remove all pieces of tape.

3. Glue sepia-pesto paper to the 12"-square paper.

4. Apply sepia ink to the face of the playing card. Apply old-photograph-brown ink over the edges of the playing card. Cut the 8½" x 11" black paper to slightly larger than the playing-card-sized photograph. Glue the photograph to the black paper. Glue the matted photograph to the center of the playing card. Glue the card to the upper-right side of the page.

5. Print text onto the 8½" x 11" white paper. Cut the text from the paper. Apply sepia ink to the edges of the text. Glue the text to the left-hand side of the page. Glue a photograph to the upper-right area of the text paper.

6. Cut excess black scrapbook paper to slightly larger than the third photograph. Glue the photograph to the black paper. Use foam dots to attach the matted photograph to the page. Glue the military medal photocopies to the page.

7. Cut a figure from the remaining photograph and glue to the lower-right corner of the page.

EDWARD MARCHELITIS

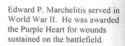

Edward P. Marchelitis served in World War II. He was awarded the Purple Heart for wounds sustained on the battlefield.

Serving in 2 Platoon 1st Battalion Company A 407 Infantry, 102nd Infantry Division, he was awarded two bronze stars for valor. One due to his injury and the other for serving in the infantry. During WWII, the infantry saw the harshest conditions.

Antique Page

Materials

- 7½" x 10½" piece of white scrapbook paper
- 8½" x 11" sheet of white scrapbook paper
- 8½" x 11" sheets of black scrapbook paper (3)
- Archival paper glue
- Craft scissors
- Flower rubber stamp
- Inks in carnation pink, sepia, tea-stain brown, and walnut stain
- Number rubber stamps
- Photographs
- Pink paper roses
- Polyester fiberfill
- Ruler

Instructions

1. Create a fold in the lower-left corner of the 7½" x 10½" paper. Tear off pieces from the upper-left corner and from the right-hand edge of the paper.

2. Use polyester fiberfill to apply tea-stain ink to the paper. Apply sepia ink to the edges of the tea-stain paper. Apply walnut stain ink over the torn edges of the paper.

3. Cut a narrow strip from an 8½" x 11" black paper to 10½" long. Glue the strip vertically to the left-hand side of the antiqued page. Cut a second strip from black paper to 7½" long. Glue this strip horizontally to the upper part of the antiqued page.

4. Choose a date that relates to the photographs. Use walnut ink to stamp the date onto the upper-right area of the antique paper.

5. Glue the antiqued page to a second 8½" x 11" black paper.

6. Cut the remaining 8½" x 11" black paper to slightly larger than the two photographs. Glue photographs to the pieces of paper. Glue the pieces to the page.

7. Use carnation pink ink to stamp the flower image onto the 8½" x 11" white paper. Apply carnation pink ink over the flower. Cut out the flower. Glue the flower to excess black scrapbook paper. Cut out the image, leaving a narrow black border around the flower. Glue the flower to the upper right of the page. Glue the pink paper roses to the lower left of the page.

Rose Vines

Materials

- ⅛"-wide pink ribbon
- 7½" x 10½" piece of white scrapbook paper
- 8½" x 11" sheet of vellum paper
- 8½" x 11" sheets of black scrapbook paper (2)
- Archival paper glue
- Clear gel craft glue
- Computer and printer, or marker
- Craft scissors
- Crayon
- Cream paper rose
- Inks in carnation pink, sepia, and tea-stain brown
- Low-tack masking tape
- Photograph
- Polyester fiberfill
- Rose vine stencil
- Seed beads
- White lace
- White tag

Instructions

1. Use low-tack masking tape to create a ½" border around the four edges of the 7½" x 10½" paper. Use polyester fiberfill to apply tea-stain brown ink to the paper. Apply carnation pink ink to the four edges of the paper.

2. Use low-tack masking tape to secure the rose vine stencil to the paper. Apply sepia ink to the stencil. Remove the stencil. Carefully remove the tape.

3. Apply tea-stain brown ink to the edges of the white tag. Use clear gel craft glue to adhere the lace to the tag. Use archival paper glue to adhere the paper rose to the tag. Apply three dots of clear gel craft glue to the lace. Press the tip of a crayon onto a seed bead. *Note: The crayon helps to grab the seed bead and makes it easier to transfer.* Place the seed bead onto the lace. Repeat with remaining seed beads. Attach the ribbon to the tag hole.

4. Use archival paper glue to adhere the rose vine background paper to an 8½" x 11" black paper.

5. Cut the remaining 8½" x 11" black paper to slightly larger than the photograph. Glue the photograph to the black paper, then glue the matted photograph to the center of the rose vine paper.

6. Glue the tag below the photograph.

7. Print text onto the vellum paper. Tear the text from the vellum paper. Glue the vellum paper to the upper left of the page.

Zachary John Fiehl, a gentle man, built this house for his loving wife, Anna Hortage-Fiehl. Daughter, Nancy, is standing in front of their barn in the back yard.

ZACHARY JOHN FIEHL

Stamped Stars

Materials

- 8½" x 11" sheet of black scrapbook paper
- 8½" x 11" sheet of white scrapbook paper
- 11"-square piece of white scrapbook paper
- 12"-square sheet of black scrapbook paper
- Archival paper glue
- Computer and printer, or marker
- Craft scissors
- Inks in meadow green and sepia
- Low-tack masking tape
- Photographs (3)
- Polyester fiberfill
- Star rubber stamp

Instructions

1. Use low-tack masking tape to create a ½" border around the four edges of the 11"-square paper. Place two horizontal strips of low-tack masking tape across the top and bottom of the paper, leaving a 1"–2" area between the tape and the top or bottom of the page. Use polyester fiberfill to apply meadow green ink to the 1"–2" areas. Remove the horizontal pieces of masking tape. Lightly apply sepia ink over the entire paper.

2. To create the dark green lines on the paper, apply two vertical strips of low-tack masking tape at the left-hand side of the paper, leaving ⅛" between the strips. Apply meadow green ink over the exposed ⅛" area. Remove the vertical strips of masking tape. Use the same process to create a horizontal line below the stamped area of the paper. Remove the horizontal strips of masking tape.

3. Use sepia ink to stamp the star image over just the sepia area of the paper. Continue to stamp the star onto the paper until the entire area is covered. Remove the tape from the edges of the paper.

4. Glue the background paper to the 12"-square paper.

5. Print the page title and text onto the 8½" x 11" white paper. Cut the title and text from the paper. Glue the title to the bottom of the page.

6. Cut excess white scrapbook paper to slightly larger along the top and side edges than one photograph. Leave sufficient space below for text. Glue the photograph to the white paper, then glue the text below the photograph.

7. Cut the 8½" x 11" black paper to slightly larger than the white photograph/text paper. Glue the white photograph/text paper to the black paper, then glue to the left-hand side of the page.

8. Glue remaining photographs to the page as desired.

Faded Stripes

Materials

- 8½" x 11" sheet of black scrapbook paper
- 8½" x 11" sheet of vellum paper
- 8½" x 11" sheet of white scrapbook paper
- Archival paper glue
- Computer and printer, or marker
- Inks in crimson red, pesto green, sepia, and walnut stain
- Low-tack masking tape
- Photograph
- Polyester fiberfill

Instructions

1. Use low-tack masking tape to create a ³⁄₄" border around the four edges of an 8½" x 11" white paper. Place two strips of low-tack masking tape horizontally across the paper, spacing them evenly.

2. Use polyester fiberfill to apply pesto green ink to the top and bottom exposed areas. Apply sepia ink over the pesto green areas.

3. Apply crimson red ink onto the exposed area in the center of the paper. Apply sepia ink over the crimson red ink. Carefully remove the tape.

4. Create a dark brown border on the edge of the page by placing a piece of masking tape ¹⁄₈" in from the left-hand side of the paper. Apply walnut stain ink to the edge. Carefully remove the tape. Repeat this process on the remaining three edges of the page.

5. Cut an 8½" x 11" black paper to slightly larger than the photograph. Glue the photograph to the black paper. Glue the piece to the center of the faded stripe paper.

6. Print text onto vellum paper. Cut text from the vellum paper. Glue vellum text above the photograph.

1950s Blue

Materials

- 4" x 11" piece of scrap paper with torn edges
- 6" x 8½" piece of black scrapbook paper
- 7½" x 10½" piece of white scrapbook paper
- 8½" x 11" sheet of black scrapbook paper
- 8½" x 11" sheet of vellum paper
- Archival paper glue
- Bingo card
- Computer and printer, or marker
- Craft scissors
- Inks in sepia and true blue
- Low-tack masking tape
- Newspaper clipping
- Photographs (2)
- Polyester fiberfill

Instructions

1. Use low-tack masking tape to create a ¼" border around the four edges of the 7½" x 10½" paper. Place the scrap paper ½" from the top of the background paper. Use polyester fiberfill to apply true blue ink to the area between the stencil and the upper area of the background paper. Move the stencil down the page ½" and apply the ink above the stencil again. Continue down the page in this manner.

2. Apply sepia ink over the entire background paper.

3. Glue the blue paper to the 8½" x 11" black paper.

4. Glue the 6" x 8½" paper to the center of the blue paper. Print text onto the vellum paper. Tear text from the vellum paper. Glue the vellum text over the black paper.

5. Glue the photographs and newspaper clipping over the black paper.

6. From the bingo card, cut out numbers that make up the year relating to the photographs. Glue the numbers to the upper right of the page.

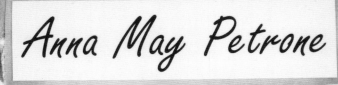

Anna May Petrone

School Photo: Age 6. Borrowed beads from her sister, Elizabeth for the photo. The dress was red and Anna's mother added the color and trim to the dress.

Confirmation photograph. Anna May, age 10

Confirmation photograph. Anna May, age 10. Brother, Anthony, age 11.

Vintage Rose

Materials

- ¼" hole punch
- 2½" x 10½" strip of white scrapbook paper
- 8½" x 11" sheet of black scrapbook paper
- 8½" x 11" sheet of white scrapbook paper
- 10½"-square piece of white scrapbook paper
- 11"-square piece of white scrapbook paper
- 12"-square sheet of black scrapbook paper
- Archival paper glue
- Computer and printer, or marker
- Craft scissors
- Inks in carnation pink, meadow green, and sepia
- Large butterfly rubber stamp
- Large flower rubber stamp
- Photographs (3)
- Polyester fiberfill
- Rosebud stencil

Instructions

1. Use polyester fiberfill to apply carnation pink ink to the 10½"-square paper. Apply sepia ink to all four edges of the paper.

2. Stencil a rosebud pattern over the 2½" x 10½" strip of white scrapbook paper, using carnation pink for the roses and meadow green for the leaves and stems. Apply meadow green ink to the edges of the strip.

3. Glue the 11"-square paper to the 12"-square paper. Glue the carnation pink paper to the 11"-square paper. Glue the rosebud strip vertically to the center of the pink carnation paper.

4. Cut the 8½" x 11" black paper to slightly larger than one photograph. Glue the photograph to the black paper, then glue the matted photograph to the center of the page.

5. Glue a photograph to the upper left of the page. Glue the remaining photograph to the lower right of the page.

6. Print the page title onto the 8½" x 11" white paper. Cut the title from the paper. Cut a piece from excess white scrapbook paper to slightly larger than the title paper. Apply carnation pink ink to the larger paper. Glue the title to the pink paper. Glue the piece to the upper right of the page.

7. Stamp flowers and a butterfly onto excess white scrapbook paper with carnation pink ink. Cut out the images. Glue the images to the page.

8. Apply carnation pink ink to excess white scrapbook paper. Punch 10 circles from the paper. Glue eight circles to the page. Glue two circles to the center of the flowers.

7

Miniature Albums, Cards, and Embellishments

Accordion Flag Book

Materials

- ⅓" x 31" white ribbon
- 1⅝" x 5" pieces of white scrapbook paper (9)
- 4"-square photographs (2)
- 6"-square pieces of black scrapbook paper (4)
- 6" x 10" piece of white scrapbook paper
- 8½" x 11" sheet of white scrapbook paper
- 12"-square sheet of black scrapbook paper
- 12"-square sheets of white scrapbook paper (2)
- Archival paper glue
- Computer and printer, or marker
- Craft scissors
- Feather rubber stamp
- Ink in meadow green
- Photograph to fit on cover
- Ruler

Instructions

1. Use polyester fiberfill to apply meadow green ink to a 12"-square white paper. Use the meadow green ink to randomly stamp the feather image over the entire paper.

2. Fold the 6" x 10" paper accordion-style into eight sections that are approximately 1½" wide. *Note: This folded section will be the spine of the book.*

3. Sandwich and glue one end fold of

the 6" x 10" folded spine between two 6"-square papers. Sandwich and glue the remaining end fold between the remaining two 6"-square papers.

4. Open the book and lay it flat. *Note: The white spine should form three peaks.* Starting on the left side of the book, glue a $1^5/_8$" x 5" strip of paper to the top front of the first peak. Glue a second strip to the lower front of the first peak. Glue a third strip to the back of the first peak, centering it between the first and second strips. Continue this process on the remaining peaks of the spine until all nine strips are used. *Note: These are the flags of the book.*

5. Lay the book flat and stretch it so the top and bottom flags are facing toward the right. *Note: The center flags should be facing toward the left.* Tear the green background paper into nine $^3/_4$" x $4^1/_2$" strips. Glue the pieces to the center of each of the nine flags.

6. Print text onto the $8^1/_2$" x 11" paper. Glue the text over the green background strips.

7. Cut the 12"-square black paper to slightly larger than each of the photographs. Glue the photographs to the black paper. Cut the green background paper to slightly larger than each of the matted photographs. Glue the matted photographs to the green background papers. Cut a 12"-square white paper to slightly larger than each of the green background papers. Glue the green background papers to the white papers. Glue the layered photographs to the inside covers of the book.

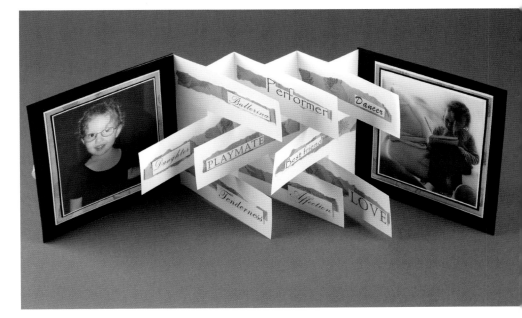

8. Glue the ribbon horizontally to the center of the front cover. Glue a layered photograph over the ribbon. *Note: To tie the album closed, bring the left-hand end of the ribbon around the back of the album, then tie with the right-hand end of the ribbon.*

Accordion Flag Card

Materials

- 3⅝" x 4⅝" pieces of white scrapbook paper for the inside covers (2)
- 3¾" x 4⅝" pieces of white scrapbook paper (2)
- 4" x 5" pieces of black scrapbook paper for the front and back covers (2)
- 4⅝" x 9" piece of white scrapbook paper

- 12"-square sheet of black scrapbook paper
- 12"-square sheet of white scrapbook paper
- Archival paper glue
- Clear gel craft glue
- Cranberry marker
- Ink in meadow green
- Ivy stencil

- Photographs (5), any size smaller than 3⅝" x 4⅝"
- Polyester fiberfill
- Ruler
- Silver brad
- Wire cutters

Instructions

1. Use polyester fiberfill to apply meadow green ink to the 12"-square white paper. Place the ivy stencil over the paper. Use meadow green ink to stencil the ivy image onto the paper. Remove the stencil. Use a cranberry marker to add a dot pattern over the stenciled images.

2. Fold the 4⅝" x 9" paper accordion-style into six sections that are approximately 1½" wide. *Note: This folded section will be the spine of the card.*

3. Use archival paper glue to adhere one end fold of the folded spine between the 4" x 5" front cover and the 3⅝" x 4⅝" inside cover. Sandwich and glue the other end fold of the spine between the remaining two pieces of the black back cover and the white inside cover.

4. Open the book and lay it flat. The white spine should form two peaks. Glue a 3¾" x 4⅝" paper to the front of the first peak. Glue the remaining 3¾" x 4⅝" paper to the front of the second peak.

5. Tear two pieces of the green ivy stenciled paper to 3" x 12". Glue the green ivy stenciled paper along the bottom of the inside of the card.

6. Cut the 12"-square black paper to slightly larger than each of the photographs. Glue the photographs to the pieces of black paper. Glue the photographs to the front and insides of the card.

7. Clip the ends from the silver brad with wire cutters. Use clear gel craft glue to adhere the silver brad to the front cover.

Accordion Family Tree Book

Materials

- 5" x 6¼" pieces of black scrapbook paper (2)
- 5" x 12" pieces of white scrapbook paper (4)
- 8½" x 11" sheet of black scrapbook paper
- 8½" x 11" sheets of white scrapbook paper (2)
- Archival paper glue
- Craft scissors
- Cream eyelets (2)
- Decorative paper punches (optional)
- Fabric leaves (3)
- Flower rubber stamp
- Inks in banana yellow, crimson red, meadow green, old-photograph brown, and tea-stain brown
- Leaf rubber stamp
- Photographs (10–12), any size smaller than 2½" x 4½"
- Polyester fiberfill
- Rose embroidery thread
- Ruler
- Silver heart charm
- Stickers (optional)

Instructions

1. Use crimson red ink to stamp the flower image onto an 8½" x 11" white paper. Stamp the leaves using meadow green ink. Use polyester fiberfill to apply banana yellow ink over the entire paper. Apply tea-stain brown ink over the yellow ink. Cut the paper into 2½" x 4½" pieces.

2. Fold and crease parts of the remaining 8½" x 11" white paper. Apply tea-stain brown ink to the paper. Lightly apply old-photograph-brown ink to the paper. Cut the paper into 2½" x 4½" pieces.

3. Fold each 5" x 12" paper accordion-style, until each strip has four 3"-wide sections. Glue these strips of paper together, gluing one strip's 3"-wide end fold on top of the next strip's 3"-wide end fold. Continue in this manner until you have an approximately 36"-long accordion. *Note: This will become the inside of the book.*

4. Fold each 5" x 6¼" paper in half. *Note: These two pieces will become the front and back covers of the card.*

5. Sandwich and glue one white end fold between the folded black front cover. Sandwich and glue the remaining white end fold between the black back cover.

6. Fasten an eyelet to the front cover, at the center of the outside edge. Repeat for the back cover. Thread rose embroidery thread through each hole. Tie a knot to secure the thread in each hole.

7. Use the 2½" x 4½" yellow or brown papers and pieces cut from the 8½" x 11" black paper to create a collage for each page of the book. Add family photographs, family tree information, and other desired embellishments, such as decorative paper punches or stickers, to the collages. Glue each collage to the inside pages of the book.

8. Create a collage on the front cover of the book with a photograph and other desired embellishments and text. Glue three fabric leaves to the upper-right side of the front cover. Attach the silver heart charm to the rose embroidery thread.

Envelope Memory Album

Materials

- ⅛" x 7" rose-colored ribbon
- ¼" hole punch
- 2¾" metal fastener
- 4" x 6" piece of white scrapbook paper (4)
- 4¾" x 6½" pink envelopes (4)
- 6¼" x 6¾" pieces of lack scrapbook paper for the front and back covers (2)
- 8½" x 11" sheet of black scrapbook paper

- 8½" x 11" sheet of white scrapbook paper
- 12"-square sheet of black scrapbook paper
- Archival paper glue
- Computer and printer, or marker (optional)
- Craft scissors
- Floral stencil
- Inks in aqua, carnation pink, and meadow green

- Low-tack masking tape
- Photographs (9)
- Pink heart charm
- Polyester fiberfill
- Ruler
- Silver heart charm

Instructions

1. Use a piece of low-tack masking tape to secure the floral stencil to the 8½" x 11" white paper. Use a small piece of polyester fiberfill to apply carnation pink and aqua ink over the flower areas of the stencil. Apply meadow green ink to the leaves of the stencil. Carefully remove the masking tape and floral stencil.

2. Cut each envelope flap so that 1¼" remains from the base of the envelope flap. *Note: The 1¼" flap will become the spine of the book.*

3. Place the envelopes between the 6¼" x 6¾" papers. Use the 2¾" metal fastener as a guide for where you will need to punch the ¼" holes on the left-hand side of the album. Punch the holes in the cover and envelope spine. Insert the metal fastener to secure the pages. Thread the rose-colored ribbon through the holes near the metal fastener. Secure the ribbon with a knot. Tie the silver and pink heart charms onto each ribbon end.

4. Glue a photograph to the front cover of the album.

5. Choose four photographs to go on the front of the envelopes. Cut the 8½" x 11" black paper to slightly larger than each of these photographs. Glue the photographs to the black papers. Cut the stenciled background paper into four pieces that measure 4" x 5½". Glue the stenciled background papers to each of the four photographs. Glue the matted photographs to the front of each envelope page.

6. Glue the remaining photographs to the back of the envelope pages.

7. Cut the 12"-square paper into four pieces slightly larger than the 4" x 6" papers. Glue the white papers to the black papers. Decorate each of the cards with photographs or text. Insert cards into the envelopes.

Fan Album

Materials

- ¼" hole punch
- 2" x 12" strip of black scrapbook paper
- 8½" x 11" sheets of black scrapbook paper (3)
- 8½" x 11" sheets of white scrapbook paper (2)
- 12"-square sheet of white scrapbook paper
- Archival paper glue
- Clear gel craft glue
- Craft scissors
- Decorative brad
- Feather rubber stamp
- Inks in banana yellow, clear embossing, cobalt blue, and crimson red
- Old earring
- Polyester fiberfill
- Ruler
- Silver heart charm
- Silver metallic pigment powder
- Small photographs (6)
- Spray fixative
- Talc-free baby powder
- Text rubber stamp
- Thread
- Typewriter alphabet stickers
- White tags (3)

Instructions

1. Use polyester fiberfill to randomly apply banana yellow, crimson red, and cobalt blue inks to the 12"-square paper. Use crimson red ink to stamp the text image over the entire paper. Dust the paper with talc-free baby powder. Use clear embossing ink to randomly stamp the feather image onto the paper. Dust the images with silver metallic pigment powder. Spray the images with fixative.

2. Fold the 2" x 12" strip of paper in half. *Note: The folded edge of the paper is the bottom of the album. The open edge of the paper is the top of the album.* Punch a hole at the top of the album. Cut a section from the multicolored paper to smaller than the cover. Use archival paper glue to adhere the paper onto the album cover. Cut a strip from the multicolored paper. Glue the strip to the right-hand side of the cover. Apply typewriter stickers to the bottom of the strip of paper.

3. Cut an 8½" x 11" black paper into four pieces slightly smaller than the cover. Cut an 8½" x 11" white paper into four pieces slightly smaller than the black pieces of paper. Glue the white pieces of paper to the black pieces of paper. *Note: These are the base pages for the album.*

4. Cut the multicolored background paper into four equal strips smaller than the base pages. Cut four pieces from the remaining 8½" x 11" white paper to slightly larger than the multicolored strips. Glue the white paper to the multicolored strips.

5. Cut four pieces from an 8½" x 11" black paper to slightly larger than the white pieces from Step 4. Glue these black pieces to the back of the white pieces. Glue the black papers to the album's base pages. Add text as desired onto the base page.

6. Cut four pieces from the remaining 8½" x 11" black paper to slightly larger than the photographs for the base pages. Glue the photographs to the black papers. Glue the photographs to the album's base pages.

7. Punch a hole in the top of each of the base pages, making sure the holes are all at the same point. Insert the pages inside the album's cover, aligning all the holes. Use a decorative brad to secure the covers and the base pages. Glue the remaining photographs to the face of the tags. Use clear gel craft glue to adhere a silver heart charm to the face of the tags. Use thread to tie the tags to an old earring. Glue the earring to the decorative brad.

Tag Album

Materials

- ¼" hole punch
- 2¾" x 6" pieces of black scrapbook paper (2)
- 8½" x 11" sheet of black scrapbook paper
- 8½" x 11" sheets of white scrapbook paper (3)
- Adhesive foam dots
- Archival paper glue
- Clear gel craft glue
- Computer and printer, or marker
- Craft scissors
- Cream eyelets (4)
- Eyelet setter
- Fabric leaf
- Feather rubber stamp
- Inks in banana yellow, cobalt blue, meadow green, orange, and tea-stain brown
- Jump ring
- Metal brad
- Photographs (5–10)
- Polyester fiberfill
- Round corner punch
- Ruler
- Silver heart charms
- Square tag
- Tiny bricks (optional)
- White thread
- Wire embellishments (optional)

Instructions

1. Use polyester fiberfill to apply meadow green ink to an 8½" x 11" white paper. Use cobalt blue ink to randomly stamp the feather image over the entire paper.

2. Apply banana yellow ink to an 8½" x 11" white paper. Randomly apply orange ink over the banana yellow ink. Randomly apply meadow green ink to some areas of the paper. Apply a light coat of tea-stain brown ink over the entire paper. Cut this paper into four 2¾" x 6" rectangles. Use a round corner punch to create rounded corners on the tags. Create a collage on each of the orange tags, using photographs, wire embellishments, tiny bricks, or any other desired embellishments.

3. Print text onto the remaining 8½" x 11" white paper. Cut text from the paper. Cut a piece from the green background paper to slightly larger than the text. Use archival paper glue to adhere the text to the green background paper. Cut the 8½" x 11" black paper to slightly larger than the green background paper. Glue the black paper to the green background paper. Using an eyelet setter, secure the cream eyelets to the tops of the tags. Add a cream eyelet to the bottom of the longest tag. Use a jump ring to attach a silver heart charm to the eyelet.

4. Create a small hole in the bottom of the square tag. Use a jump ring to attach a silver heart charm to the square tag. Use foam dots to attach the fabric leaf to the square tag. Tie all the tags together using the white thread.

5. Use a round corner punch on the corners of the 2¾" x 6" papers. *Note: These are the covers of the tag book.* Punch a hole in the top of each orange tag and black cover. Use a metal brad to secure the tags and covers together.

6. Select a photograph for the cover. Tear the green background paper to larger than the photograph. Glue the green background paper to the front black cover. Glue the cover photograph to the center of the green paper.

7. Attach the tags to the back of the metal brad.

Text Tag

Materials

- 8½" x 11" sheet of black scrapbook paper
- 8½" x 11" sheets of white scrapbook paper (2)
- Archival paper glue
- Computer and printer, or marker
- Craft scissors
- Cream eyelets
- Cream roses (optional)
- Eyelet setter
- Ink in banana yellow
- Polyester fiberfill
- Silver heart charms (optional)
- White knitting yarn

Instructions

1. Use polyester fiberfill to apply banana yellow ink to an 8½" x 11" white paper.

2. Print text onto the remaining 8½" x 11" white paper. Cut out the text. Cut pieces from the banana yellow paper to slightly larger than the text. Glue the text papers to the banana yellow papers.

3. Cut the 8½" x 11" black paper to slightly larger than the banana yellow background papers. Glue the banana yellow papers to the black papers.

4. Using the eyelet setter, secure a cream eyelet to the top of each tag. Thread white knitting yarn through the eyelets and tie in a knot. Embellish the tags with cream roses or silver heart charms, if desired.

Butterfly Tag

Materials

- ⅛" x 12" rose-colored ribbon
- 1" x 2" blue ribbon
- 4"-square pieces of white scrapbook paper (3)
- 8½" x 11" sheet of white scrapbook paper
- Archival paper glue
- Butterfly rubber stamp
- Computer and printer, or marker
- Craft scissors
- Cream eyelets (3)
- Detail embossing powder in silver
- Embossing heat tool
- Eyelet setter
- Flower rubber stamp
- Heart stencil
- Inks in aqua, carnation pink, clear embossing, meadow green, purple, and true blue
- Oval tag
- Photograph
- Polyester fiberfill
- Ruler
- Silver heart charm
- Square tag

Instructions

1. Place the heart stencil onto a 4"-square paper. Use polyester fiberfill to apply true blue ink to the heart stencil several times until the paper is covered.

2. Lightly apply carnation pink ink onto a second 4"-square paper. Use carnation pink ink to randomly stamp the flower image over the paper.

3. Use clear embossing ink to stamp the butterfly image onto the remaining 4"-square paper. Sprinkle silver detail embossing powder onto the butterfly. Shake off the excess powder. With the embossing heat tool, heat the embossing powder on the paper.

4. Apply aqua, meadow green, and purple ink over the butterfly. Cut out the butterfly image.

5. Glue the pink background paper to the oval tag. Glue the butterfly image onto the lower part of the oval tag. Cut a figure from the photograph and glue over the butterfly. Using the eyelet setter, secure a cream eyelet to the tag hole.

6. Cut the blue background paper to 1⅛" square. Glue the blue background paper to the upper-left corner of the square tag. Cut the pink background paper to ¾" x 1". Glue the pink background paper to the upper-right corner of the square tag.

7. Print text onto the 8½" x 11" paper. Cut the text from the paper.

8. Glue the blue ribbon to the bottom of the square tag. Glue the text over the blue ribbon. Using the eyelet setter, secure a cream eyelet to the top and bottom of the square tag.

9. Thread the rose-colored ribbon through the eyelets on the tags. Tie a loop in the top of the ribbon. Tie the silver heart charm to the bottom of the ribbon. For added stability, glue the ribbon to the back of the tags if desired.

Trifold Miniature Album

Materials

- 3½" x 11½" piece of white scrapbook paper
- 4" x 12" piece of black scrapbook paper
- 8½" x 11" sheet of white scrapbook paper
- Archival paper glue
- Computer and printer, or marker
- Cream eyelets (2)
- Eyelet setter
- Flower paper punch
- Ink in meadow green
- Light green embroidery thread
- Low-tack masking tape
- Photographs (5)
- Pliers
- Polyester fiberfill
- Ruler
- Silver heart charm

Instructions

1. Tear a 7" piece of low-tack masking tape in half. Place the first half of the tape diagonally across the lower-left corner of the 3½" x 11½" paper. Place the second half of the tape diagonally across the upper-right corner of the paper.

2. Use polyester fiberfill to apply a light coat of meadow green ink to the upper and lower corners of the paper. Carefully remove the masking tape.

3. Fold the 4" x 12" paper in thirds accordion-style so that each section measures 4" square.

4. Glue the white and green background paper to the center of the folded black scrapbook paper. Using the eyelet setter, attach an eyelet on the front outside edge and back outside edge.

5. Glue photographs to the green background paper. Print text onto the 8½" x 11" paper. Cut out the text sections and glue them to the green background paper.

6. Punch out nine flowers from excess white scrapbook paper. Glue the flowers to the white and green paper.

7. Use pliers to attach the silver heart charm to the back eyelet. Thread the light green embroidery thread through both eyelets. Tie each of the threads into a knot.

Primitive Deer

Materials

- ³⁄₄"-square piece of white scrapbook paper
- ³⁄₄" x 1¹⁄₄" piece of white scrapbook paper
- 2¹⁄₂" x 3³⁄₄" piece of white scrapbook paper
- 4¹⁄₂" x 5¹⁄₂" piece of cream scrapbook paper
- 7" x 10" piece of black scrapbook paper
- 8¹⁄₂" x 11" sheet of white scrapbook paper
- Acrylic paint in gold
- Archival paper glue
- Clear gel craft glue
- Green eyelash ribbon
- Inks in Prussian blue & sepia
- Low-tack masking tape
- Paintbrush
- Polyester fiberfill
- Primitive deer rubber stamp
- Scrap paper
- Swirl rubber stamp

Instructions

1. Place strips of masking tape randomly on the 2¹⁄₂" x 3³⁄₄" paper. Use polyester fiberfill to apply sepia ink onto the exposed areas of the paper. Carefully remove the tape. Apply a light coat of sepia ink over the entire paper. Tear a piece from scrap paper and place the torn edge diagonally across the lower-right corner of the paper. Use sepia ink to darken the lower-right side of the paper. Remove the torn paper. Use sepia ink to stamp three primitive deer over the patterned background.

2. Apply Prussian blue ink to the ³⁄₄"-square paper. Use gold paint to stamp the swirl onto the square. Paint the ³⁄₄" x 1¹⁄₄" paper with gold. Glue the blue square to the gold rectangle.

3. Fold the 7" x 10" paper in half to create a 5" x 7" card. Cut the 8¹⁄₂" x 11" paper to slightly smaller than the black paper. Fold the white paper in half, then glue it to the inside of the card.

4. Glue the 4¹⁄₂" x 5¹⁄₂" paper to the front of the card.

5. Glue the patterned background paper to the center of the cream paper. Glue the blue/gold embellishment to the lower-right corner of the patterned background paper. Use clear gel craft glue to adhere the green eyelash ribbon to the left-hand side of the black folded paper.

Biography Box

Materials

- ⅛" x 9" gold ribbon
- 3½"-square pieces of white scrapbook paper (5)
- 3"–4"-square cream box
- 8½" x 11" sheets of white scrapbook paper (2)
- Archival paper glue
- Computer and printer, or marker
- Craft scissors
- Faux pearls (15")
- Floral stencil
- Inks in aqua, carnation pink, meadow green, tea-stain brown
- Low-tack masking tape
- Miniature frame
- Paper doily (optional)
- Photographs
- Polyester fiberfill
- Quick-drying craft glue
- Ruler
- White roses (10)

Instructions

1. Use a piece of low-tack masking tape to secure the floral stencil onto an 8¹⁄₂" x 11" white paper. Use a small piece of polyester fiberfill to apply carnation pink and aqua ink over the flower parts of the stencil. Use meadow green ink to stencil the leaves.

2. Carefully remove the masking tape and the floral stencil. Lightly apply tea-stain brown ink over the entire paper.

3. Use archival paper glue to adhere a 3¹⁄₂"-square paper to the top of the box. Cut the floral background paper to 3" square. Glue this paper to the center of the 3¹⁄₂"-square paper.

4. Use quick-drying craft glue to adhere the miniature frame to the center of the box top. Glue the gold ribbon to the sides of the frame. Fill the center of the frame with white roses. Glue faux pearls around the floral background paper to hide the edges.

5. Apply tea-stain brown ink to both sides of the remaining 3¹⁄₂" squares. Glue photograph collages to the front of each square.

6. Print biographies onto the remaining 8¹⁄₂" x 11" paper. Cut out each biography and glue it to the back of each square. *Note: If the biography text is much smaller than the back of the square, fill the space with the lace edge from a paper doily.*

Blue Mountains

Materials

- 4" x 5¼" piece of white scrapbook paper
- 4" x 5¼" pieces of silver paper (3)
- 5½" x 7½" piece of white scrapbook paper
- 8" x 12" piece of black scrapbook paper
- 8½" x 11" sheet of white scrapbook paper
- Acrylic paint in gold
- Adhesive foam dots
- Archival paper glue
- Black photograph corners (4)
- Inks in cobalt blue and crimson red
- Jump ring
- Leaf rubber stamp
- Photograph
- Polyester fiberfill
- Scrap paper
- Silver heart charm
- Tiny hole punch

Instructions

1. Place a piece of scrap paper diagonally across the 4" x 5¼" white paper, allowing the upper-right corner to be exposed. Use polyester fiberfill to apply a heavy coat of cobalt blue ink to the corner. Move the scrap paper slightly down the paper and tilt it to the left. Apply a lighter coat of cobalt blue to the exposed area of the paper. Move the scrap paper slightly down the paper and keep it tilted to the left. Repeat the same process, using crimson red ink. Continue the process until the entire page is covered.

2. Use gold paint to stamp the leaf design in the center of the paper. Attach two silver papers to the back of the blue/red paper.

3. Fold the 8" x 12" paper in half to make a 6" x 8" card. Cut the 8½" x 11" paper to slightly smaller than the piece of black paper. Fold the white paper in half, then glue to the inside of the card.

4. Use the black photograph corners to attach the 5½" x 7½" paper to the front of the black folded paper. Glue the blue mountain background paper to the center of the white paper.

5. Cut a piece from the remaining silver paper to slightly larger than the photograph. Glue the photograph to the silver paper. Punch a tiny hole in the bottom of the photograph. Use a jump ring to attach the silver heart charm to the hole in the photograph. Use foam dots to secure the photograph to the lower-right corner of the blue/red paper.

D'Arte Card

Materials

- 2¼"-square piece of vellum paper
- 4" x 5½" piece of black scrapbook paper
- 5" x 7" blank white card
- 8½" x 11" sheet of white scrapbook paper
- Archival paper glue
- Clock face rubber stamp
- Craft scissors
- Inks in crimson red, old-photograph brown, and sepia
- Jump rings
- Photograph
- Ruler
- Silver heart charm
- Swirl rubber stamp
- Tiny hole punch
- Typewriter alphabet sticker

Instructions

1. Glue the 4" x 5½" paper to the front of the blank card.

2. Stamp the clock with old-photograph-brown ink onto the 8½" x 11" paper. Use polyester fiberfill to apply sepia ink over the stamped clock. Cut out the clock. Glue the clock to excess white scrapbook paper. Cut out the image, leaving a narrow white border all around the clock.

3. Cut a ¼" x 1¼" piece from excess white scrapbook paper. Apply crimson red ink onto the paper. Use the crimson red ink to stamp the swirl image onto the paper.

4. Cut a rectangle from excess white scrapbook paper to 2⅛" x 3¾". Cut a curve in the bottom of the rectangle. Punch three tiny holes in the bottom of the rectangle.

5. Cut three small strips from excess white scrapbook paper. Punch a hole at one end of each of the strips. Attach the strips to the curved rectangle with jump rings. Attach a silver heart charm to one of the strips.

6. Glue the photograph to the 2⅛" x 3¾" paper. Tear a corner from the vellum and glue to the top edge of the photograph. Tear another corner from the vellum and glue to the bottom edge of the photograph.

7. Glue the crimson red rectangle horizontally to the bottom of the curved rectangle. Glue the curved rectangle to the black paper.

8. Cut the stamped clock in half. Glue the clock above the curved rectangle. Apply a typewriter sticker just above the photograph.

About the Author

As an artist and writer, Carol Heppner's work appears in well-known national publications. Her signature is to explore new techniques and media in the arts-and-crafts industry. Her work is novel and sophisticated, but the techniques are straightforward with readily available materials.

Carol works in a wide range of mediums including book arts, digital collage, photography, polymer clay, scrapbooking, stained glass, and wearable arts. Carol's passion for genealogy research provides a base for much of her artwork. Her Italian-inspired, polymer clay masks and mixed-media collages have appeared in galleries and in art shows.

During the past ten years, Carol's articles have helped strengthen the content of publications such as *Belle Armoire, Somerset Studio, Scrap and Stamp Arts, Expression Magazine, Rubber Stamper,* and *Handcrafted: The Best Art Projects of Stampington & Company.* Carol has also contributed work in the following books: *Stamp Artist Project Book, Rubber Stamped Jewelry, Lazertran Art Project Book,* and *Polymer Clay Stamped Jewelry Book.* She is on the editorial advisory board of *Scrap and Stamp Arts,* Scott Publications, and is a design member of the Crafts and Hobby Association (CHA).

Carol, a native of Archbald, Pennsylvania, currently lives in New Jersey with her husband Paul.

Acknowledgments

Writing this book has been a thrill and a huge undertaking all wrapped into one. I am grateful to Chapelle for the opportunity to bring readers the techniques and projects that will make for many hours of pleasure. Many thanks to those at Chapelle for recognizing the connection between my art techniques and the desire by many to quickly create sophisticated scrapbook pages. I also appreciate the guidance of Cindy Stoeckl and Lisa Anderson from Chapelle in their tireless efforts to bring all of these projects together into a book.

Writing a book is not done in a vacuum. There are so many people who graciously gave of their time, their materials, and their photographs. I appreciate the loving support and the many hours my husband Paul worked to proofread the first drafts of this book. I am very blessed to have such a wonderful loving partner to share my life.

I am very grateful to Anne Generas of Ranger Industries, who generously supplied all the Pigment, Archival, Adirondack, Tim Holtz's Distress, and Nick Bantock Dye inks and adhesive foam dots used in this book. Many thanks also to Linda Bagby of Duncan, who generously supplied the Aleene's Memory, Quick Dry Tacky, Clear Gel Tacky Glue, and Fast Grab Tacky glues, as well as the solid stamps that were used in the projects. I am appreciative to Kim Meyers of Jacquard, who generously supplied Pearl Ex pigment powders and Lumiere paints; and to Jennifer O'Byrne of Fairy Tale Scrapbook Creations, who generously supplied the stencils, stickers, and vellum embellishments seen on the art projects in this book. The beautiful overall-patterned stencils used in many projects are the compliments of the staff at Delta, Inc.

My brother Paul Marchelitis was a tremendous source of moral support and constant teasing throughout the entire process of this book. I also very much appreciate the contributions of all family and friends who appear in these pages. Also, many thanks to Lori and Robert Childs, Ann Gifford-Carozzi, Kathy Heppner, Mary Jane and Paul Heppner, Pasquale Lopetrone, Ed Marchelitis, Geraldine and Anthony Petrone, Lucille Taylor, Annie and Ralph Smith, and Marty and Greg Smith for the use of their wonderful photographs.

Finally, I offer my appreciation to my good friends and colleagues Sharilyn Miller (Stampington & Co.) and Kelly Philage (Scrap and Stamp Arts). Both Sharilyn and Kelly have provided the venues by which my artistic creations transcend from worktable to printed page.

Metric Conversion Chart

mm-millimeters   cm-centimeters
inches to millimeters and centimeters

inches	mm	cm	inches	cm	inches	cm
⅛	3	0.3	9	22.9	30	76.2
¼	6	0.6	10	25.4	31	78.7
½	13	1.3	12	30.5	33	83.8
⅝	16	1.6	13	33.0	34	86.4
¾	19	1.9	14	35.6	35	88.9
⅞	22	2.2	15	38.1	36	91.4
1	25	2.5	16	40.6	37	94.0
1¼	32	3.2	17	43.2	38	96.5
1½	38	3.8	18	45.7	39	99.1
1¾	44	4.4	19	48.3	40	101.6
2	51	5.1	20	50.8	41	104.1
2½	64	6.4	21	53.3	42	106.7
3	76	7.6	22	55.9	43	109.2
3½	89	8.9	23	58.4	44	111.8
4	102	10.2	24	61.0	45	114.3
4½	114	11.4	25	63.5	46	116.8
5	127	12.7	26	66.0	47	119.4
6	152	15.2	27	68.6	48	121.9
7	178	17.8	28	71.1	49	124.5
8	203	20.3	29	73.7	50	127.0

yards to meters

yards	meters	yards	meters	yards	meters	yards	meters	yards	meters
⅛	0.11	2⅛	1.94	4⅛	3.77	6⅛	5.60	8⅛	7.43
¼	0.23	2¼	2.06	4¼	3.89	6¼	5.72	8¼	7.54
⅜	0.34	2⅜	2.17	4⅜	4.00	6⅜	5.83	8⅜	7.66
½	0.46	2½	2.29	4½	4.11	6½	5.94	8½	7.77
⅝	0.57	2⅝	2.40	4⅝	4.23	6⅝	6.06	8⅝	7.89
¾	0.69	2¾	2.51	4¾	4.34	6¾	6.17	8¾	8.00
⅞	0.80	2⅞	2.63	4⅞	4.46	6⅞	6.29	8⅞	8.12
1	0.91	3	2.74	5	4.57	7	6.40	9	8.23
1⅛	1.03	3⅛	2.86	5⅛	4.69	7⅛	6.52	9⅛	8.34
1¼	1.14	3¼	2.97	5¼	4.80	7¼	6.63	9¼	8.46
1⅜	1.26	3⅜	3.09	5⅜	4.91	7⅜	6.74	9⅜	8.57
1½	1.37	3½	3.20	5½	5.03	7½	6.86	9½	8.69
1⅝	1.49	3⅝	3.31	5⅝	5.14	7⅝	6.97	9⅝	8.80
1¾	1.60	3¾	3.43	5¾	5.26	7¾	7.09	9¾	8.92
1⅞	1.71	3⅞	3.54	5⅞	5.37	7⅞	7.20	9⅞	9.03
2	1.83	4	3.66	6	5.49	8	7.32	10	9.14

Index